SELF-WORKING
TABLE MAGIC

97 FOOLPROOF TRICKS WITH EVERYDAY OBJECTS

Karl Fulves

With 185 Illustrations by Joseph K. Schmidt

Dover Publications, Inc.
New York

Self-Working Table Magic; 97 Foolproof Tricks with Everyday Objects is a new work, first published by Dover Publications, Inc., in 1981.

International Standard Book Number: 0-486-24116-5
Library of Congress Catalog Card Number: 80-69257

Manufactured in the United States of America
Dover Publications, Inc., 31 East 2nd Street, Mineola, N.Y. 11501

INTRODUCTION

The quickest, most certain path toward achieving a reputation of being a magician is to be able to perform at a moment's notice with borrowed objects. If you are handed a coin, a handkerchief, a pencil or a rubber band, you should be able to do at least one amazing trick with that object. This book deals exclusively with just such tricks. It is a collection of some of the best tricks with ordinary objects.

Some chapters have been designed to present the reader with a complete act of close-up magic. For example, the chapter entitled "Magic Show in a Matchbox," gives you about 15 minutes worth of excellent tricks and stunts to amaze and amuse your audience. The chapter closes with a jumping match and a match penetration, two of the strongest illusions in close-up magic, and ones that should guarantee you a round of applause from your audiences.

Not considered here are tricks with lit matches, lit cigarettes or knives, on the theory that you shouldn't risk being burned or cut doing magic tricks. But you will find in this book magic with many other objects, from eggs to dice, from cards to balloons, from apples to whisk brooms. There are even tricks done with mirrors.

Magic is the most entertaining hobby because it offers surprise and mystery. When magic is properly presented it will delight and baffle your audiences. Master the tricks in this book and you will be ready to entertain anytime, anywhere, with some of the finest of all close-up mysteries.

A special note of thanks is due Martin Gardner and Joseph K. Schmidt for their assistance in compiling material for this book.

CONTENTS

MONEY MAGIC

Everyone carries coins. If you know a few coin tricks, you are always in a position to entertain people with coin magic. The tricks in this chapter represent a collection of some of the best coin routines done without sleights or specially prepared apparatus.

1. QUICKSILVER

Ask for the loan of a quarter. When you get the coin, remark that some coins of this particular date, unknown to most people, have a low melting point. As a result, the coin has a curious property which you now demonstrate.

The coin is placed under a handkerchief. Immediately the coin melts through the center of the handkerchief. Both the coin and the handkerchief may be borrowed, and the coin may be marked.

METHOD: The trick is accomplished by means of a clever turnover move with the handkerchief. But note that when you borrowed the quarter, you made it seem that the coin was the key element in the trick because it had a low melting point. By making up this story, you focused attention on the coin and therefore away from the handkerchief.

This is the element of misdirection. Audience attention is directed to the object that has very little to do with the working of the trick. In this case the audience will concentrate attention on the coin and forget about the handkerchief. This is all to the good since the coin has nothing to do with the secret working.

Have the spectator note the date on the quarter. You can even have him mark the quarter. When the marked coin is returned to you, hold it between the right thumb and forefinger.

Then drape a handkerchief over the right hand. Pinch a bit of the fabric with the right thumb. The situation at this point is shown in Figure 1.

The left hand grasps the end of the handkerchief that is toward the audience and brings it back onto the right arm, thus exposing the coin to the audience's view, as shown in Figure 2.

It is here that the trickery comes into play. The left hand releases its grip on the end of the handerchief. The right hand then lowers with a quick snapping motion so that the handkerchief assumes its original position, Figure 3.

But although this *seems* to be the original position, with the coin under the handkerchief, the coin is actually outside the handkerchief as indicated in Figure 4. Thus the trick is over before the audience knows what you are going to do.

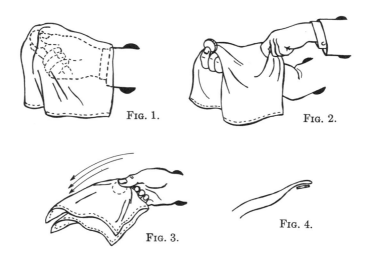

Fɪɢ. 1.   Fɪɢ. 2.

Fɪɢ. 3.   Fɪɢ. 4.

Twist the handkerchief around the coin a few times with the left hand. Then, while the left hand holds the handerchief, the right hand slowly pulls the coin out into view. It appears as if the coin penetrates the center of the handkerchief. The handkerchief can be returned unharmed to the spectator.

"The MacCarthy Hank Fold," described later in this book, allows you to perform the same trick by a different but highly ingenious method.

2. MYSTERY VANISH

In this surprising trick you have a spectator hold a penny and a nickel on his outstretched palm. Explain that you will tap either coin with a pencil and that this coin will immediately vanish.

He indicates a coin, say the penny. You tap it with the pencil, but instead of the penny vanishing, the *pencil* vanishes! The pencil is later found in the pocket.

METHOD: Ask a spectator to remove a penny and another coin from his pocket. Explain that this will work only if one coin is copper and the other silver. Have him place the two coins side by side on his outstretched right palm.

Tell him that he can choose either coin, and that simply by tapping the coin with the pencil, you will cause it to vanish. Thus you will never touch the coin directly, yet the coin will disappear.

Say he indicates the penny. Tap the pencil against the coin and then move the pencil up in an arc as shown in Figure 5. The coin hasn't vanished, so you tap the coin again. This time bring the right hand further up so it moves past the right side of the face.

Again nothing happens. Tap the coin again. This time bring the right hand up quickly and leave the pencil behind the right ear, Figure 6.

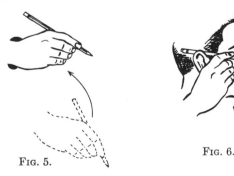

FIG. 5.

FIG. 6.

Without pause say, "One more try." Immediately bring the right hand down as if to tap the coin, but act amazed that the pencil has vanished. If you stand with your left side slightly toward the spectator, or with the face turned slightly to the right, he won't see the pencil behind the ear and thus will be astonished that the pencil has completely vanished.

To produce the pencil magically, direct attention away from yourself. The best way to do this is to point to the floor behind the spectator and say, "There it is." As the spectator turns his back to you, remove the pencil from behind the ear and drop it in your pocket.

The spectator can't find the pencil. Act puzzled. Pat your pockets, then pretend to have suddenly discovered the whereabouts of the illusive pencil. Remove it from the pocket. Done smoothly, it is a bewildering sequence.

3. GHOST COIN

This trick and the next one nicely routine together. The first trick depends on an *audible* illusion, while the second exploits a *visible* illusion to produce the desired mystery.

In this first routine the spectator drops a coin into a glass. The coin instantly penetrates the glass. All articles may be borrowed.

METHOD: The trick depends on the sound a coin will make when it drops into a glass. Hearing this sound, the audience assumes the coin is in the glass. As is always the case with magical effects, things are not quite as they seem because the coin is actually outside the glass.

Place a coin under a handkerchief. Ask a spectator to grip the coin through the cloth. Ask him, "Did you notice that they're making glasses thinner and thinner these days? Let me show you."

Pick up a glass and place it mouth-up on the outstretched left palm. Direct the spectator to lower the handkerchief over the glass. Then tell him to release the coin so it falls into the glass. He *hears* it fall into the glass, so all appears fair. What you really do is this. When the handkerchief completely covers the glass, tilt the glass back at an angle, Figure 7. When the spectator releases the coin, it hits the side of the glass and falls into the left palm. Thus the coin is already out of the glass.

Ask the spectator to release the handkerchief so it is loosely draped over the glass. Grasp the glass and handkerchief with the right hand. Say, "This glass is so thin, a coin can penetrate it like this." Give the glass a shake with the right hand. At the same time, release the coin from the left palm, Figure 8. It appears as if the coin dropped right through the glass. The audience may think there is a hole or slot in the glass, but of course nothing of the kind is used.

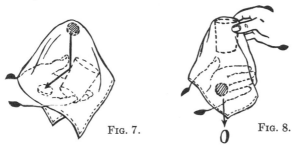

Fig. 7.   Fig. 8.

4. THE BACKWARD GHOST

If you are asked to repeat "Ghost Coin", or if you want a trick that is an ideal follow-up, "The Backward Ghost" fills the bill. After performing "Ghost Coin," say to the spectator, "I'll make it harder. First we'll pour a bit of water into the glass." Pour about an ounce or two of water into the glass.

The spectator grips the coin through the cloth. He drops it into the glass. The magician lifts the handerchief and the spectator *sees* the coin in the glass, resting at the bottom under water.

"The coin is under water so I can't tamper with it. Note that the coin is heads up." The spectator sees that the coin is heads up. "We'll cover it for a moment because these things work better in the dark."

The glass is covered with the handkerchief. When the glass is uncovered a moment later, the spectator sees that the coin is now tails up. It has turned over by itself under water!

Finally the magician covers the glass again and this time the coin instantly penetrates the glass of water.

As before, all apparatus may be borrowed and the coin can be marked. The spectator should be impressed that his own marked coin turned over by itself while under water, and then, for a bonus, penetrated the glass.

METHOD: Basically the secret is the same as in "Ghost Coin" but an extra ingredient has been added. At the start of the routine, cover the borrowed coin with a handkerchief and ask the spectator to grip the coin through the cloth.

Then pour an ounce or two of water into the glass. Hold the glass on the outstretched left palm. Direct the spectator to place the handkerchief over the glass. He releases the coin. As in Figure 7 of the previous trick, the glass is tilted at an angle, so the coin hits the side of the glass and falls into the left palm.

Have the spectator release the handerchief so it is loosely draped over the glass. Then grip the glass through the cloth and move it forward so that the glass is directly over the coin.

If you now remove the handkerchief and ask the spectator to look down into the glass, he will see the coin resting at the bottom of the glass of water. Of course this is an illusion produced by the water itself, but it looks exactly as if the coin rests at the bottom of the glass and not under it.

Ask the spectator to note whether the coin is heads up or tails up. Then cover the glass with the handkerchief. After the glass is covered, lift it slightly with the right hand, The left fingers then curl in, Figure 9. This causes the coin to turn over.

Fig. 9.

Lower the glass onto the coin again. Lift the handkerchief away. The spectator looks down into the glass and sees that the coin has mysteriously turned over while it was under water.

Cover the glass with the handkerchief. Grip the glass through the cloth with the right hand as in Figure 8, release the coin and it apparently penetrates the glass.

There is one tip that makes this routine even more baffling. When you pour water into the glass, get a few drops onto the fingers of the left hand. When the coin falls into them, transfer the moisture to the coin. Later, when the coin apparently penetrates the glass, it will be wet, exactly as if it really was in the water at the start of the trick.

5. HOLE IN THE POCKET

A quick trick with a surprise finish. The magician has a coin marked. Commenting that he has a hole in his pocket and that loose change is always falling through the hole, the magician drops the marked coin into his right trouser pocket.

"The odd thing is that the hole isn't in this pocket," the magician says. "It's in the other pocket, so when things drop through ..." Here he lifts his *left* foot to reveal the borrowed coin under that foot.

METHOD: The trick relies more on nerve than magical ability. The key to it is the use of an extra coin. We'll say the coin is a nickel. Secretly place it on the floor and cover it with the left foot. This may be easier said than done, depending on the circumstances under which you perform the trick. An easy way to prepare the trick is to have the nickel in the hand. Drop some other object, say a paper napkin, to the floor. While retrieving the napkin, leave the nickel on the floor. Then cover the nickel with the left foot.

To present the routine, ask someone for the loan of a nickel. Tell him to place a mark on it, adding, "That's so you'll recognize it if you should ever see it again."

Take the coin. Explain that you have a hole in your trouser pocket. Place the nickel in the right trouser pocket. Bring out the hand and show the hand empty. Pat or shake the trouser leg so that the nickel supposedly tumbles down the trouser leg to the floor.

Say, "The puzzling thing is that the hole is in the *other* pocket, so the nickel ends up here." As you finish this sentence, lift the left foot to reveal the nickel. It is a surprising result.

Immediately reach down with the right hand, pick up the nickel and place it in the right trouser pocket, acting as if the nickel is yours. Leave it in the pocket, but take the other nickel with the right hand. Say, "Is this nickel yours or did you give it to me?" The spectator will say that he gave it to you but that it's still his. Remove it from the pocket and return it to him. Naturally he will check the mark on the nickel.

6. SEALED SILVER

Removing an envelope from his pocket, the magician says, "Postage being what it is these days, it cost my friend twenty cents to send me sixteen cents worth of coins." The magician removes a dime, a nickel and a penny from the envelope, closes the flap and has a spectator keep it in his pocket.

"But these coins are special. They don't have to travel by mail. Let me show you." The three coins are covered with a handkerchief. When the handkerchief is removed, one coin, say the dime, is gone. The spectator then removes the envelope from his pocket, opens it and finds the dime back inside!

METHOD: There are actually four coins. Aside from the dime, the nickel and the penny, there is an extra dime. Place it inside the envelope near one corner. This is the only preparation. Put the other three coins into the envelope at the opposite side, then fold the envelope to keep the coins separate, Figure 10.

Fig. 10.

When ready to present the routine, remove the three coins, leaving the extra dime inside the envelope. Fold the envelope and place it in the spectator's jacket. Comment about these being special coins which can travel about as they choose, and at rates considerably cheaper than the postal-service charges.

Hold the three coins between the left thumb and fingertips, but with the dime a bit higher than the other two coins. The right hand then drapes a handkerchief over the coins. Snap the fingers of the right hand.

Grasp the handkerchief at the near end and draw it back so that it slides free of the coins. Nothing has happened. Place the handkerchief over the coins again, but this time grasp the dime through the cloth with the right thumb and forefinger.

This time, as the right hand draws the handkerchief back, it takes the dime with it, Figure 11, and drops the dime into the handkerchief pocket of the jacket. All attention is on the coins in the left hand, so the steal of the dime goes undetected.

Fig. 11.

Drop the nickel and penny onto the table, showing that the dime has vanished. Then direct attention to the spectator's pocket. He removes the envelope, opens it, and finds the missing dime.

7. MERLIN'S MAGIC

"Merlin, official magician to the Court of King Arthur, used a number of magic words from a book of spells. I have a copy from a recent edition of the book." So saying, the magician opens a book of spells to reveal that there is a pile of seven pennies in the middle of the book.

"Count the pennies," the magician says. "Make sure there are seven because seven is the magic number." The spectator counts the coins to verify that there are seven. The coins are then poured into the spectator's hands and he is instructed to hold them tightly.

Removing another penny from his pocket, the magician causes it to vanish. The vanish occurs openly. The coin is merely tossed into the air and it evaporates. The spectator holding the coins may be standing some distance away. He is asked to catch the invisible coin that the magician just vanished.

The spectator makes a catching motion. He then opens his hands and counts the pennies. Where there were originally seven, now there are eight. The magician's penny joined the other seven while they were tightly held in the spectator's own hands.

METHOD: There are really two secrets involved here. The first is the method of vanishing the penny, and the second is the method of causing it to appear in the spectator's hands.

We shall begin with the method of causing the penny to appear in the spectator's hand. Get a book on black magic or astrology. Open it to the center and place seven pennies on the center page. Slide an extra penny into the spine of the book and then close the book. Have the book handy on a nearby table at the start.

When ready to perform, open the book to the page where the pennies are. Ask a spectator to count them. He will of course count seven pennies. Have him hold his cupped hands together as you slide the pennies off the book and into his hands. In the process, the extra coin in the spine of the book is secretly added, Figure 12. Thus, unknown to the spectator, he really has eight coins. Tell him to close his hands tightly around the pennies.

MAGICIAN

FIG. 12.

Now reach into your pocket and remove a handful of coins. With the other hand pretend to remove a penny. In fact you remove nothing. Just hold the hand as if it contained a coin. Return the rest of the change to the pocket.

Make a tossing motion, as if tossing a coin into the air toward the spectator. The supposed coin in your hand vanishes, seemingly into thin air. Some people may even say later that they saw the coin evaporate into the air.

The spectator holding the pennies opens his hands and counts how many pennies he has. He started with seven, but now he has eight.

Once, as a gag, I used a spelling book and introduced it as a book of spells. The same gag can be used with a dictionary if you explain that it contains all the words to magic spells, though not necessarily in the right order. In any event, just make sure the book has a hardcover and that the opening in the spine is large enough to comfortably take the extra coin.

8. THE ESCAPE ARTIST

This baffling trick will even fool magicians, yet it is easy to do. The only constraint is that you must perform it for someone sitting directly across the table from you. Here is the effect:

"Magicians are always accused of using their sleeves. This time I'd like to use your sleeve." So saying, the magician drops three coins down the spectator's jacket sleeve. He then causes one of the coins to penetrate the spectator's sleeve. Only three coins are used. They may be borrowed and marked. There are no gimmicks and there is no sleight of hand.

METHOD: The secret is audacious but simple. It depends primarily on presentation so we will detail the handling as thoroughly as possible. First, remember that the spectator should be seated directly across the table from you. The routine works best for one spectator. If others are present they might see how the trick is done.

Ask to borrow three coins. The coins may be marked by the spectator, or he can simply remember the date on each coin. Make it clear that your hands are empty, your sleeves rolled up. It is assumed the spectator is wearing a jacket.

Say to him, "Since magicians are accused of using their sleeves, for this trick I'm going to use *your* sleeve." Hold the three coins in your right hand as you speak. The right elbow rests on the table, Figure 13.

ELBOW ON TABLE → Fig. 13.

"I'd like you to place your arm like this." The presentation is important here. As you say, ". . . like this," rest your left arm on the table and place your head against your left hand, Figure 14.

Fig. 14.

Since the spectator will be sitting across from you, he will likely place his *right* arm on the table and rest his head in his right hand. As he does this, say, "No, the other hand." The gesture that accompanies these words is completely natural but it is the key to the trick. Your right arm swings forward and you touch his left arm near the elbow, Figure 15. This is done to indicate that he is to use his left arm. But as you gesture in this way, simply leave behind one coin on the table near his left elbow.

Fig. 15.

Immediately your right hand swings up to its original position. The right elbow always stays in contact with the tabletop during the back and forth swings of the right arm. The spectator can't see the coin you've left behind on the table because his own arm blocks it from his view. From your point of view the trick is over, but from the spectator's perspective it has yet to begin.

Drop the two coins into the spectator's jacket sleeve as you say, "I'm going to drop these three coins into your sleeve. Since you now have them, there is no way I can tamper with the coins." Show both your hands to be unmistakably empty as you talk.

"Now the hard part. I don't know exactly which coin it will work with, but I'm going to try to cause one of those three coins to penetrate your jacket sleeve. Of course I could do it by cutting a hole in the sleeve with a pair of scissors, but it's much more puzzling to do it by magic."

With both hands grasp the spectator's left jacket sleeve near the elbow. Tug on the sleeve a bit. Pretend to examine the material as if looking for a seam. As the left hand does this, the right hand quietly picks up the coin that was secretly placed on the table.

Push this coin against the spectator's sleeve. Say, "I think I've got it," and then, with a quick pull, pretend to pull the coin out of his sleeve. He can immediately verify that the mark on the coin is his. When he removes the other coins from his sleeve he will see that there are only two and both are his.

This is a strong close-up trick, little-known, even to magicians. Spend a few minutes practicing it to get the handling down smoothly and you will be rewarded with a coin trick that will fool even sleight-of-hand experts.

9. MILLION-DOLLAR MYSTERY

We close this chapter with one of the strongest impromptu tricks with coins. Unlike the preceding tricks in this chapter, a coin does not appear, disappear or penetrate some object. Rather, this is a mind-reading trick and one of the best.

Twelve pennies are placed on the table. Some are heads up, some are tails up. While the magician turns his back, the spectator mixed up the coins by sliding them about. The coins are mixed to the spectator's satisfaction.

With his back still turned, the magician gathers six coins behind his back and gives them to the spectator to hold. The magician claims that these six coins contain as many heads-up coins as there are heads-up coins on the table, and as many tails-up coins as there are tails-up coins on the table.

The spectator checks, and it turns out that the magician is correct! The trick can be repeated with any even number of coins. The coins may be borrowed and the magician can be blindfolded.

METHOD: The trick depends on an ingenious principle devised by Bob Hummer. When you place the 12 pennies on the table, make sure that six are heads-up and six are tails-up. Scatter the coins around, then turn your back.

Direct the spectator to mix the coins further by sliding them about randomly. He can't turn them over, but he can slide them about any way he likes. When the coins have been mixed to the spectator's satisfaction, and with your back still turned, slide six of the coins toward you. Because of the ingenuity of the system, they can be any six coins.

Gather the six coins, one at a time, in your hand. Stack them one on top of the next, taking care not to accidentally turn any coin over. When you have a stack of six coins, tell the spectator to gather the other six coins and hide them by covering them with a coffee cup or a book.

Turn and face the spectator. Your stack of six coins is now behind your back. Secretly turn the stack over. Then bring the stack into view and place the six coins on the table one at a time. Remark that you have as many heads showing on your six coins as the spectator has on his, and further that you have as many tails showing as the spectator has on his coins.

The spectator lifts the coffee cup. His group of coins may show four heads and two tails. He checks your group of six coins and will be amazed to discover that it too shows four heads and two tails.

If you repeat the trick, make sure you start with six heads and six tails showing. The trick can be done with any even number of coins as long as you begin with an equal number of heads and tails.

MAGIC SHOW IN A MATCHBOX

All of the tricks in this chapter use matches, but since the matches aren't lit, you can use toothpicks instead. If you have a matchbox to carry the apparatus around in, you are ready to entertain with a magic show in a matchbox. The best way to present such a show is to do a few match puzzles, then a magic trick, then a few more puzzles, then another magic trick with matches. Thus the audience is both entertained and mystified by your show.

This chapter begins with a collection of some of the best puzzles with matches, and then concludes with a number of clever magic tricks with matches.

10. EUCLID'S TRIANGLE

Toss six matches onto the table. Tell the spectator he is to form eight triangles with the matches. He can't bend or break any match. You can even give him a time limit of one minute, but it's more fun to give him as much time as he likes. Since there are only six matches, the whole thing seems impossible anyway.

When the spectator gives up, arrange three matches in a triangle as you say, "There's one triangle." Then place the other three matches on top, saying, "And here's seven more." Referring to Figure 16, you will find two large triangles formed by the matches, plus six small triangles around the perimeter.

Fig. 16.

11. SQUARING THE SQUARE

Having shown the spectator a trick with triangles, you tell him, "Here's an easier one with squares." Actually, it's harder, but you don't tell him that. Besides, it *looks* easier at first glance. Arrange the squares as shown in Figure 17, saying, "I've done half the work for you. All you have to do is remove two matches and end up with two squares."

FIG. 17.

It's true that you've done most of the work, but the puzzle isn't as easy as it looks. Most people tend to assume that they must end up with two squares of the same size, an impossible task. When they give up, remove match A and match B from the lower left corner, producing a square inside a square.

This puzzle is a good example of the case where a person will unconsciously add constraints that were never stated in the problem, in effect backing themselves into a corner because they've only succeeded in making a simple problem impossible.

12. FOUR SQUARE

"I'll make it even easier for you. Here's five squares. You don't have to take away even one match. Just move two matches so you form four squares of the same size." Form the five squares of Figure 18 as you speak. All the spectator has to do is move two matches to make four squares, yet he should find the test quite difficult.

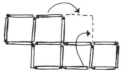

FIG. 18.

When he gives up, move two matches as indicated by the arrows in Figure 18 to get the desired solution. This is an excellent test of the powers of observation. If you are later asked to repeat the puzzle, start with the four-square configuration, and ask the spectator to move two matches and form *five* squares of equal size. Further, if you set up the matches again, but this time upsidedown, the spectator should still find it next to impossible to get the right answer.

13. THE ROMAN EQUATION

There are many match puzzles where matches are set up to form an incorrect equation. You are then asked to move matches to make the equation correct. A simple example is shown in Figure 19. The equation is incorrect as shown. To change it to a correct equation, move one match. The solution is shown in Figure 20.

But the best example I know of in this category is the one shown in Figure 21. The equation states in Roman numerals that 10 plus 1 equals 9. Obviously this is wrong. Without moving *any* matches you are required to change it to a correct equation.

$$| - ||| = || \qquad \text{Fig. 19.}$$

$$| = ||| - || \qquad \text{Fig. 20.}$$

$$X + | = | X \qquad \text{Fig. 21.}$$

The spectator is encouraged to think that if he can't move a match, the solution must lie in *removing* one match. You can even imply that he could be correct in following this line of thinking. It makes no difference because even in removing a match the stunt seems impossible.

The surprising solution is that the spectator doesn't move a match, he moves himself. By moving around to the other side of the table he will see the equation upside down, and in this form it is correct.

14. A FISH STORY

This elegant match puzzle is of Oriental origin. Arrange eight matches and a match head to form the fish shown in Figure 22.

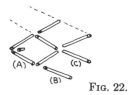

Fig. 22.

Note that the fish is swimming to the left. The match head is the fish's eye. By moving three matches and the match head, reverse the direction of the fish so it is swimming to the right.

The distracting element here is the fact that the matches do indeed form the *shape* of a fish, so it would appear difficult to cause the *entire* fish to change direction. But by moving matches A, B, C, to the position shown by the dotted lines in Figure 22, plus the match head, the fish does indeed change direction, Figure 23.

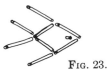

Fig. 23.

15. TIPSY COCKTAIL

Use four matches to form a cocktail glass, and a match head for the olive or cherry, Figure 24. Without touching the olive, move two matches and cause the olive to end up outside the cocktail glass.

This puzzle combines two different features in its solution. Of the two matches you move, one is picked up and transferred to a new location, while the other is slid to a new location. It is therefore unlikely that the spectator will catch on to the answer too quickly. The solution is shown in Figure 25. The cocktail glass is now upside down, but the olive is outside the glass.

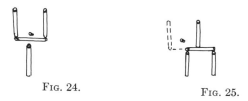

Fig. 24.

Fig. 25.

16. THE LITTLE HOUSE

Youngsters are fascinated with match puzzles. The following is one of the oldest, but is little known and quite intriguing to children. Using 15 matches, form the house shown in Figure 26. Explain that a little girl lives in the house. The spectator is to move five matches to reveal her name and her age.

The solution is shown in Figure 27.

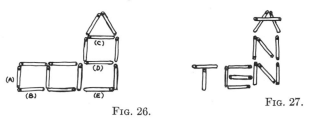

Fig. 26.

Fig. 27.

17. WORLD'S STRONGEST?

"It is all well and good to show off your strength by lifting hundreds of pounds, but suppose the object weighed less than an ounce. Would you have trouble lifting a match packet?" So begins the patter for this curious feat of strength.

Begin by placing a match packet or matchbox on the table in front of an upright cigarette package. If no cigarette pack is handy, stand a cased deck of cards on its long end and use that. Then grasp the matchbox between your first finger and third finger as shown in Figure 28. Using just these two fingers, and

Fig. 28.

keeping the middle finger in contact with the tabletop at all times, the problem is to lift the matchbox and place it on top of the cigarette pack. Figure 29 shows the end result.

Fig. 29.

It will seem simple until you try it and then it will seem impossible. But keep at it for a few minutes and you will acquire the knack. It is really a test of coordination. Mentally you must direct two fingers to perform a task they have not been trained to do. With just a small amount of practice you will find that it becomes easy to do. Not only that, but once the knack is acquired, you do not have to practice it again, Once learned, the stunt is never forgotten.

If you do the stunt enough, sooner or later you will meet someone who knows how it is done, or who, through sheer persistence, acquires the knack. When this happens, you switch to a method devised by me. As soon as you see the person succeed with the stunt, say, "I made a mistake. You don't grip the matchbox between the first and third finger. You grip it between the middle finger and little finger."

It looks like the same stunt but *now* it has become a real challenge. Most people give up because they think it really is impossible. But if you practice this method you will acquire the knack. Learn to do both methods with either hand. If the spectator succeeds in doing it with his right hand, say to him, "Did I make another mistake? I meant for you to do it with your *left* hand. Like this." At this point the struggling spectator is sure to give up.

18. WHO PAYS THE BILLS?

You are in a restaurant and it's time to pay the bill. Say, "Let's play a little game. The loser pays the bill." Take a handful of matches or toothpicks. Break them in half and drop them into a hat, cup or an envelope.

Remove a half-match. Then the spectator removes a half-match. Continue this way, taking turns. The person who has to remove the last half-match must pay the bill.

Make sure you go first and you will always win. It makes no difference how many matches are used. This "betcha" was a favorite of Nate Leipzig. For a variation, if the fellow sitting across from you insists on going first, say to him, "Now remember that you can remove only one at a time, like this." Reach into the hat or cup and remove a half-match as if to illustrate what he is to do. Then give him the opportunity to go first. Of course he will lose.

19. MATCHING MATCHES

This is a fine mental effect with matches or toothpicks. We will assume you use a box of about 30 matches. The number is not important. The magician removes some matches and counts them. The spectator then removes some matches but he does not count them. No one knows how many matches he has.

The magician says, "If I give you two matches, then I will have as many as you plus enough more to make 16."

The magician gives the spectator two matches. Then the spectator counts his matches. Say he has eight. The magician counts 8 matches from those he holds, then counts the remainder singly, counting "9, 10, 11, 12, 13, 14, 15, 16." The sixteenth match is indeed the last match he holds, so his prediction is correct.

The trick can be repeated. Although the magician never knows how many matches the spectator holds, although the outcome is different every time, the magician is always correct in his prediction.

Method: When you remove a handful of matches from the box, make sure you remove more than half. As an example we will assume the box contains 30 matches and that you remove 16 matches:

Count the number of matches you hold. In this case you will count 16. Subtract two, getting 14. Have the spectator remove some matches from the box. Ask him to leave some behind so that you don't know the exact number he has.

Say to him, "If I give you two matches, then I'll have as many as you plus enough more to make exactly 14." Give him two matches. Then have him count his matches. As he does, you count yours in unison. He may have eight. You have counted eight from your hand. Continue counting and you will find that you have six more, exactly enough to bring your total to 14.

Another example may be useful. Again we'll assume there are 30 matches in the box. Remove more than half. Then have the spectator remove some of the remainder. Count your matches. Whatever the total, you always subtract two. Let's say you have 18 matches. Subtract two, giving you 16.

Say, "If I give you two matches, I'll have as many as you plus enough to bring my total to 16."

Hand over two matches. The spectator then counts his matches. Say he has 11. You count in unison, counting 11 matches onto the table. You then continue counting matches, beginning where you left off, saying, "12, 13, 14, 15, 16." The sixteenth match will be your last, and again your prediction is correct.

If it all seems puzzling as to *why* the trick works, note that you aren't predicting anything. What you're really doing is announcing in an indirect way how many matches you have. Thus, when you say, "If I give you two matches, I'll have as many as you plus enough more to bring my total to 16," you are really telling the spectator that you have 16 matches. It's as simple as that, but so subtle in the wording that it will fool people even if you repeat the trick.

20. THE JUMPING MATCH

This strange trick almost falls into the category of psychic magic. A matchstick is placed on the table. Another match is held in the right hand. The magician says he will concentrate psychic energy into the match in his hand and will then discharge this energy to the other match.

After a moment of concentration, the magician places the charged match near the other match, Figure 30. The audience hears a loud snap as the psychic energy is discharged, and then sees the tabled match suddenly jump into the air. It is an eerie effect.

Fig. 30.

Method: The match is held as shown in Figure 31. It must be held firmly between the right thumb and first finger, and the third finger or little finger must apply pressure to the bottom of the match.

Fig. 31.

With the match gripped in this way, pretend to concentrate, saying you will project psychic energy into the match in your hand. After a suitable time, place the match against the match on the table as shown in Figure 30.

Nothing happens. Say you will concentrate harder. Take the match away, pretend to concentrate, then place the match in hand against the match on the table so that the match heads contact one another.

Release pressure with the little finger, allowing the match in hand to flick against the match on the table. The result is that a snap will be heard as the match in hand frees itself from the little finger. The match on the table will jump back several feet.

If you do not get a loud snap, press against the match in the right hand with the fingernail of the little finger. As the nail flicks off the end of the match, a loud snapping noise will be produced. To conceal the method from the audience, make sure that the audience is at the left of the set-up as shown in Figure 30. Then they have no chance of catching the very slight movement of the right little finger.

21. THE PENETRATING MATCHES

We will close this chapter with one of the finest close-up illusions with matches. A match is held in each hand. Without gimmicks, the matches visibly penetrate one another. The trick is repeated under the closest scrutiny, yet the matches seem to magically melt through one another. I am indebted to Martin Gardner for the following description of this elegant routine.

The right hand holds its match vertically. The match is clipped at the top between the first and second fingers. The bottom of the match rests against the right thumb. The left hand holds its match horizontally. The starting position is shown in Figure 32.

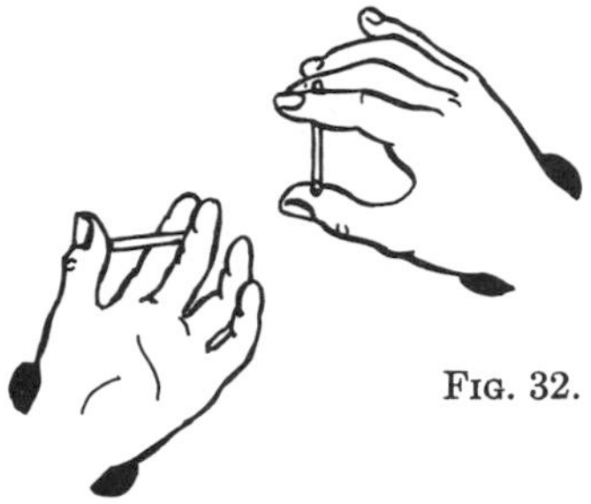

FIG. 32.

For maximum visibility the second, third and fourth fingers of each hand should be extended. The right hand is about 12 inches to the right of the left hand and about 6 inches higher. It is brought down in a slanting direction toward the left-hand match.

The secret to the trick is this. As soon as the right hand starts to move, raise the first and second fingers slightly. This creates a small gap between the end of the match and the thumb, Figure 33.

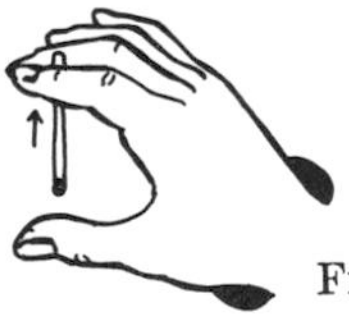

FIG. 33.

The match in your right hand then apparently penetrates the match in your left. Actually the right hand's match slides over the left hand's match, the left hand's match passing through the gap created between the right hand's match and the right thumb. As soon as the matches reach the position shown in Figure 34, the right first and second fingers press the match against the thumb to close the gap. At no time during this action does the left hand move.

Fig. 34.

As soon as the penetration is complete, reverse the moves and the matches will unlink. The trick can be repeated once again.

There are a few points that should be emphasized to enhance the illusion. First, the audience should be toward your left so they have the clearest view of the apparatus. Next, the path taken by the right hand's match should be more toward the audience than to the left. Practice this in front of a mirror to get the idea.

Practice the moves until you can reduce the gap to less than a quarter of an inch. When presenting the routine, grip the matches as in Figure 32, then tap the center of the right hand's match against the center of the left hand's match. Explain that you will try to cause the matches to penetrate one another.

Separate the hands and then produce the penetration. Reverse the move, causing the matches to unlink, then repeat the penetration again. If you want to finish impressively, do the penetration two or three times very quickly. These rapid penetrations take place because you allow the gap to remain open.

The handling suggested here can be done with large kitchen matches or toothpicks. The larger the objects, the more visible the trick. With attention paid to the details given above, you will find this a startling close-up illusion.

DICE DEXTERITY

Like the magician's control over a deck of cards, the gambler's ability to control dice is seen as a demonstration of extraordinary sleight of hand. Yet many of the best tricks and stunts with dice are easy to do if you know the secret. Dice are available in many dice games and board games, but if you carry two or three dice in your pocket you will always be ready to present the mysteries described in this chapter.

22. DICE CATCH

"Gamblers have to practice warm-up exercises just as concert pianists do. They both manipulate the ivories, but in the gambler's case the ivories are dice. Here is one of their most difficult exercises."

The magician places two dice against a glass or dice cup and holds them as in Figure 35. The idea is to toss each die in the air and catch it in the glass. The magician tosses the first die in the air and catches it in the glass. Then he tosses the second die and catches it too in the glass.

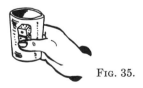

Fig. 35.

The spectator, remembering the magician's comment that this was one of the gambler's "most difficult exercises," will usually say that there's nothing at all difficult about it. He will believe it's easy until he actually tries the stunt. Then he finds that while he can catch the first die in the glass, he can't catch the second die without the first one falling out.

METHOD: The secret is this. Toss the first die in the air and catch it in the glass. But when you are ready to repeat with the second die you alter the handling in a subtle way. Raise the glass so it is at about eye level. Then, instead of tossing the second die, release it and quickly lower the glass to catch the second die in the cup.

The spectator will not notice that you have altered the handling, and unless he is lucky, he will find it next to impossible to catch the second die without the first die falling out of the glass.

23. CONTROLLED DICE SHOT

After performing the previous stunt the magician remarks, "Now that I've done the warm-up, let me show you how gamblers control fair dice. There are six numbers on each die, a total of 36 different ways two dice can be thrown. I'll bet you even money that I'll throw a one-spot or a six-spot on every roll."

Pick up the two dice, throw them and have someone keep count with pencil and paper how often a one-spot or a six-spot shows up. Since there are six different numbers on each die, it would appear that you have only two chances in six of throwing a one or a six. Actually the odds are five in nine that you will succeed, so you will win more than half the time.

Since the real odds are contrary to common sense, most people think you are cheating or using loaded dice to win the bet. Sooner or later someone will tell you he thinks you're cheating and will ask if the bet works with two other numbers. It makes no difference which numbers you choose, but don't admit to this. Instead, tell the spectator you've never tried it with other numbers, but you're willing to give it a try with, say, a three-spot and a five-spot. Roll the dice. Now you'll find that either a three-spot or a five-spot (or both) will start showing up more than half the time.

If someone accuses you of using sleight of hand, tell him that you will attempt to control the dice *while he throws them*! Hand him the two dice. It will appear impossible to laymen, because even though the spectator throws the dice, a three-spot or a five-spot shows up more than half the time. It is on the basis of simple secrets such as this one that reputations are established.

24. THE THIRTEENTH TURN

This puzzling mystery uses only one die. It is the invention of Martin Gardner. The magician draws a square on a piece of paper and places a die on the square. He asks the spectator to give the die a quarter-turn, then another and another, and so on until he has given the die 12 quarter-turns. Then he is asked to silently choose whether or not to give the die a thirteenth quarter-turn. All of the turning of the die takes place with the magician's back turned.

The spectator gives the die a thirteenth turn or not. He does it silently and does not tell the magician whether or not he gave the die the thirteenth turn. Then the magician turns around and immediately tells the spectator whether he made the thirteenth turn.

METHOD: The trick depends on what is known as a parity principle. Place a die on a sheet of paper and draw a square around the base of the die as shown in Figure 36. Note the three faces

FIG. 36.

of the die that you can see. In the illustration they are a one-, a two-, and a three-spot. Add them together and simply remember whether the total is odd or even. In our example the total is six, an even number, so we say that the parity is even.

Turn your back. Ask the spectator to give the die a quarter-turn. He can turn the die forward, back, to the left or to the right when he makes the quarter-turn. After he has given the die a quarter-turn, he slides it back to the square you drew on the paper.

Have him give the die another quarter-turn, then another, and so on until he has given the die a total of 12 quarter-turns. After each quarter-turn he slides the die back to the square on the paper without turning the die.

After he has given the die 12 quarter-turns, ask him if he wants to give the die a thirteenth turn. He makes up his mind but does not tell you his decision. Silently he may or may not give the die that last turn.

Turn around and look at the die. Add up the three visible faces. If the total is the same parity as when you started, the spectator did not give the die a thirteenth turn. In other words, if the total was even at the start and the new total is even, the die was not given a thirteenth turn. In our example the total was even at the start. If the total is even at the finish, the spectator did not give the die the thirteenth turn.

If the parity changes from even to odd or from odd to even, the spectator did give the die the 13th turn. Thus if the total was even at the start and odd at the finish, the spectator did give the die a thirteenth turn.

25. SPELL-A-DIE

After inventing the above routine, Martin Gardner devised a startling new presentation for the principle. Write the name WASHINGTON on one slip of paper and the name LINCOLN on another. Place the die on the table in front of the spectator. Turn your back. Ask the spectator to mentally decide whether he would vote for Washington or Lincoln.

Whatever his choice, he spells out the letters in that person's name, silently giving the die a quarter turn for each letter. When he has finished, you turn around, glance at the die and immediately tell him who he voted for!

METHOD: The trick works on the same principle. If the parity changes from odd to even or from even to odd, the spectator voted for Lincoln. Otherwise he voted for Washington.

By way of a specific example, place the die on the table. Say the three faces you can see are the 4, 5, and 6. The total is 15, an odd number, so the parity at the start is odd.

Turn your back. Have the spectator choose either name and mentally spell it while giving the die a quarter-turn for each letter. When he has finished, turn around and glance at the die. Total the three numbers you now see. If the total is still odd, the spectator voted for Washington. If the total is even, the spectator voted for Lincoln.

You can gain an insight into how it works by considering a simpler case. Place a coin on the table and note whether it is heads up or tails up. Then turn your back and have a spectator turn the coin over 12 times. He then decides whether or not he wants to turn the coin over a thirteenth time.

You then turn around and tell him if he turned the coin the thirteenth time. Simply note whether or not the same side is showing as was showing at the start. If it is, the spectator did not give the coin a thirteenth turn. If the opposite side of the coin is showing, the spectator gave the coin a thirteenth turn. The trick is too obvious in this form, but presented with a die, the fact that the parity changes with each quarter-turn of the die is well concealed. It is an excellent close-up mystery.

26. THE NEW DROPOUT

The basic effect is well known to magicians, but a twist has been added which makes this stunt new. Three dice are held between the thumb and middle finger as shown in Figure 37.

FIG. 37.

The problem is to allow the center die to fall to the table without allowing either of the other two dice to fall.

Unless you know the secret, it is an exceedingly difficult stunt to accomplish. The method is that beforehand you secretly moisten the thumb and first finger. Now grasp the dice as shown in Figure 37. When you release pressure the center die will fall, but the end dice will remain in place due to the moisture.

The new approach is to use four dice, preferably three of one color and one of a contrasting color. Stack them as in Figure 38. The problem is to release the center die and simultaneously catch the odd-color die so that you finish as shown in Figure 39.

The secret is exactly the same. Moisten the thumb and first finger before you begin. The knack for performing the release

Fig. 38.

Fig. 39.

and catch can be learned in just a few tries. But although you make it look simple, the spectator will think it's impossible.

If you want to practice a real test of timing and coordination, stack *two* odd-color dice, one on top of the other, then try to catch the uppermost of these between the other two dice.

27. TECHNICOLOR DICE

Required are three dice and three slips of paper. The dice have to be of different colors, say red, white, and blue. Dice of different colors are usually available in stationery and novelty stores.

In this routine the dice are thrown and the numbers added as described below. Although you have no way of controlling the way the dice are thrown, the total of the numbers always matches a prediction you wrote before the trick began.

The slips of paper are filled out as shown in Figure 40. While your back is turned, each spectator takes a slip. It makes no difference who gets which slip of paper. The dice are then thrown on the table.

Fig. 40.

Ask one of the spectators to note the two colors on the slip he holds. The colors may be red and white, though this is unknown to the magician. The spectator mentally totals the numbers on the red and white die and jots them on a slip of paper.

The next spectator now has his turn. Say his slip has white and blue written on it. Instruct him to turn over those two dice so that a fresh set of numbers shows up. Then he notes the total of the numbers on the white and blue die and jots this on the pad.

The third spectator may have the slip reading blue and red. He turns both of these dice over to bring up a fresh set of numbers. Then he notes the total of these two numbers and jots this total on the pad.

Finally the three numbers written on the pad are totaled up. Once a grand total is arrived at, the pad is turned writing-side down. The magician turns around and removes a prediction from his pocket. The prediction reads, "The total will be 21." The pad is turned over and indeed the total is 21, exactly matching the prediction.

METHOD: Follow the above handling exactly as written and the total will always be 21. The principle at work in this trick is that opposite faces on any die always total seven. In the above trick you are in essence adding together the top faces of the three dice, turning the three dice over and adding the bottom faces. Since this is three times seven, the total must be 21. But the simple principle is well-concealed in the handling.

If three different-color dice are not available, use three dice of the same color, but place them in numbered squares on a sheet of paper as shown in Figure 41. The slips of paper then refer to "Die No. 1 and Die No. 2," "Die No. 2 and Die No. 3," and "Die No. 3 and Die No. 1." The handling is otherwise the same.

FIG. 41.

28. MENTAL DIE

This routine can be done with a die or with any cube that has something different on each of the six faces. For example, you can use a child's building block or alphabet block, the kind which have letters of the alphabet on three sides and pictures on the other three sides. You can even construct a color cube by making a large die from cardboard and pasting construction paper of different colors to each side. Any square or rectangular solid can be used, even a closed cardboard box, as long as each side has a different picture, color or number.

Besides the die or cube, you will need a hat or other object large enough to cover the die later on. While the magician turns his back, the spectator places the die on the table and thinks of any number on the die.

Looking at the top, front and right faces of the die as in Figure 42, the spectator notes if his thought-of number is on any of the faces he can see. If it is, the spectator gives the die a quarter-turn to the right, shown by the arrow labeled A in Figure 42. If he doesn't see his thought-of number on any of these three faces, he gives the die a quarter-turn upward (indicated by arrow B in Figure 42).

Fig. 42.

After this is done the magician pauses and then says that he does not yet have a clear impression of the thought-of number. The instruction is repeated, and the spectator again notes if the thought-of number is on any of the three faces he can see. The spectator then gives the die a quarter-turn in the appropriate direction.

Once more the magician hesitates, saying this time that he gets a mental image but it is not quite clear. The above instruction is repeated to the spectator one more time; if he can see his thought-of-number on any of the three faces visible to him he gives the die a quarter-turn to the right; otherwise he gives the die a quarter-turn upwards.

The die is now covered with a hat. The magician has never seen the die and has no idea how the die was turned. He hasn't a clue as to the thought-of number. The magician asks one question: "Did you see your thought-of number at any time on the top, front or right face of the die?"

After the spectator answers the question, the magician reaches under the hat, adjusts the die, then asks the spectator to name his thought-of number for the first time. The spectator will name it—say it is five. He himself lifts the hat and the die is seen to have the five-spot uppermost.

METHOD: Until the very end of the trick the magician does not know what number the spectator chose. When he asks if the spectator saw his number at any time, the magician listens carefully to the spectator's reply. If the spectator says "Yes," the magician reaches under the hat and gives the die a quarter-turn toward himself. If the spectator answers "No," the magician reaches under the hat and gives the die a quarter-turn to his left. In these directions it is assumed that the magician is sitting directly across from the spectator.

Actually there is only one case where the spectator will say he never saw his thought-of number, and five where he'll say that he did, so if you want to take a slight chance, don't ask any questions. Simply reach under the hat and give the die a quarter-turn toward yourself. Five times out of six the thought-of number will be on top of the die.

29. LOGIC DICE

"Logic Dice" may at first appear to be based on the same principle as "Mental Die," but in fact the principle is different. Used in conjunction with "Mental Die," this routine tends to deepen the mystery because the method is not in any way related to the one used in "Mental Die."

The spectator is given a die and a small square of cardboard bearing the notation shown in Figure 43. While the magician

FIG. 43.

turns his back, the spectator places the die in front of himself with any number uppermost. If the top number is odd, he gives the die a quarter-turn upward as shown by the arrow in Figure 43. If the top number is even, he gives the die a quarter-turn to the right as shown by the other arrow in Figure 43.

The spectator continues doing this five or six times. He is

then told to continue until the number one is uppermost on the die. When the one-spot is on top, he gives the die one more quarter-turn (always following the instructions indicated above). Clearly a random number is now on top of the die. Yet the magician, his back still turned, immediately names the number now showing on top of the die.

METHOD: Follow the above instructions, but make sure that the spectator gives the die at least five quarter-turns. Then ask him to continue giving the die quarter-turns (always following the rule on the cardboard square). He does this until the number one shows up on top, then he gives the die one more quarter-turn.

At this point, although it appears that a random number is on top, the number on top will always be the four-spot. Reveal it in a suitably dramatic manner.

As to why it works, after five quarter-turns the die will enter a closed loop in which the numbers will show up on top in the order one-four-five-six-three-two-one-etc. So if you are asked to repeat the trick, have the spectator give the die at least five quarter-turns. Then ask him to continue turning the die until the number six comes up on top. Then he gives the die one more quarter-turn according to the rule. With your back turned, announce that the number three is on top. Of course you will be right.

Note that in "Mental Die" the spectator looks at three faces of the die each time, whereas in "Logic Dice" he looks at only one. It is this point which should puzzle anyone trying to analyze the two tricks. He thinks there's a connection between the two tricks but there is none.

30. THE RED PREDICTION

We shall close the chapter on dice tricks with a trick that uses an *invisible* die. The basic idea for this ingenious trick was devised by Arthur Carter. The present routine is adapted from a routine of Dai Vernon's.

You will use a packet of six cards and the invisible die. If playing cards are not available, you can substitute slips of paper as detailed later on.

The effect is that the cards are dealt into a row. The spectator rolls the invisible die. Say he rolls an invisible two. He counts in two from one end of the row of cards. The card he arrives at will be an Ace. Opening a prediction, he reads, "You will choose the only red card." It turns out that he did indeed choose the only red card in the row.

There are many versions of this fine trick, but the following is the easiest and the best.

METHOD: The key to the trick lies in the wording of the prediction. When the prediction indicates that the spectator chose the only red card, it seems straightforward enough but it is really ambiguous. The prediction is fulfilled if the spectator chooses the only red-faced card or the only red-backed card. Since the spectator sees the trick done only once, he is never aware that there could have been another outcome.

The six cards are shown in Figure 44. All cards except the Ace of Clubs are blue-backed. The Ace of Clubs is red-backed. With the cards dealt out into the row exactly as shown, you are ready to present the routine.

Fig. 44.

Hand the spectator the invisible die. Tell him to roll the die a few times to satisfy himself that it isn't loaded. Say all of this with a straight face and the audience can't help but smile.

Now say, "I want you to roll the invisible die one more time. We'll use whatever number you roll." The spectator rolls the invisible die. Ask him what number came up. Whatever his answer, ask him if he wants to change his mind and roll the die again. Assume he says he's satisfied. The way you proceed from here depends on the number he says he rolled.

If he says he rolled a one, remark that the spectator chose the One, or, in other words, the Ace.

If he says two, count two cards from left to right, arriving at the Ace.

If three, count three cards from left to right, arriving at the 6.

If he says four, have him count in from his left, that is, from your right. He will arrive at the face-down six.

If he says five, he counts from his left, arriving at the Ace.

If six, remark that he rolled a six, so his card is the six.

Because of the way you handle the spectator's number, he can arrive only at the Ace or the Six. Whichever of these two cards he arrives at, place a coin or other small object in front of it to mark it as the selection.

If the chosen card is the Ace, turn all the other cards face-down. They are all blue-backed. Then have the prediction read. Then have the Ace turned face-down. It is the only red-backed card, so it matches the prediction.

If the spectator arrives at the Six as his selection, have the prediction read aloud, then turn all the cards face-up. The Six is the only red-faced card in the row, and once again the prediction is correct.

Whatever the outcome, when the trick is over gather the cards in a packet and place them in your pocket. Also ask the spectator for the return of the invisible die. Note that the trick depends on two sets of "outs" or alternate interpretations, the first in the selection of a card, and the second in the way it is revealed as the only red card. But because "outs" are used, the trick shouldn't be repeated for the same audience.

CONJUROR'S COLLECTION

This chapter begins with one of the oldest tricks and concludes with one of the newest. In between you will learn a startling coincidence trick involving movie stars, an animated puppet that performs an amazing balancing act, a balloon that changes color in an instant, and a remarkable bouncing apple.

The diversity of the apparatus used in these tricks should indeed prove to your audiences that you can perform magic with any object handed to you.

31. THE CUPS AND BALLS

One of the oldest conjuring feats is the trick which today is known as the cups and balls. The version described here was marketed by Carl Brema. Although the trick is done by professional magicians with metal cups and rubber balls or cork cubes, we will use three paper cups and rolled-up napkins or squares of newspaper to represent the balls.

The effect is that when a ball is placed on top of a cup, it immediately penetrates the cup. This is repeated with each of the three balls. Spectators watching the trick sometimes assume the cups are gimmicked to allow the balls to slip through them, but the secret is different and not at all obvious.

If possible, choose seven- or nine-ounce paper cups. Smaller cups are acceptable, but the larger cups are more visible to the audience. There is no preparation involving the cups. The secret lies in the use of an extra paper ball. The audience sees three balls, but really there are four. The extra ball is never seen by the audience.

To prepare the trick, nest the three cups as shown in Figure 45, with a paper ball between the bottom cup and the middle

Fig. 45.

cup. The nested set of three cups, plus the three visible paper balls are placed on the table when you are ready to start the routine.

Lift the stack with your left hand. The basic move is now performed. The right hand removes the top cup and in one continuous motion places it mouth-down on the table as shown in Figure 46. Without hesitation your right hand grasps the middle cup. Your right hand slides this cup (and the ball hid-

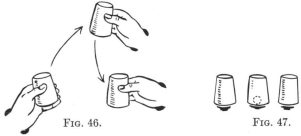

Fig. 46.

Fig. 47.

den under it) to the right and places it mouth down on the table. The ball stays under the cup due to momentum. Finally, your right hand places the last cup on the table to the right of the other two cups, Figure 47.

You have just performed the basic move. This move is the key to this version of the cups and balls, and will be used twice more during the routine. The audience is unaware that there is a ball under one of the cups.

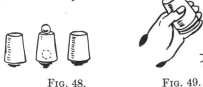

Fig. 48.

Fig. 49.

Place one of the three visible paper balls on top of the middle cup, Figure 48. Pick up the other cups, one in each hand, and nest them on top of the center cup. Snap your fingers, then lift the nest of three cups with the left hand, Figure 49, to show that the first ball has penetrated a cup.

Now place each cup on the table as you did at the beginning of the trick. That is, you perform the basic move again. The only difference is that the center cup, the one that secretly contains a paper ball, is placed directly over the paper ball on the table.

Pick up the second of the visible paper balls and place it on top of the center cup, Figure 50. Grasp each of the other cups,

FIG. 50.

one in each hand, and nest them on top of the center cup. Snap your fingers, then lift the nest of three cups with your left hand to reveal that the second ball has penetrated a cup.

Place each cup on the table as you did before, performing the basic move. The difference now is that the center cup (with the ball secretly inside) is placed directly on top of the two visible balls.

There is one visible ball left. Pick it up and say, "I'll place it in my pocket." Place the ball in your trouser pocket. But immediately bring your hand out with the fingers curled, as if you have palmed out the ball. Glance furtively at the hand. Someone is sure to say that you have a palmed ball. When they do, reply, "You caught me." Make a tossing motion with the hand toward the three cups. The ball seems to have vanished in mid-flight.

Immediately lift the center cups, revealing all three paper balls under the cup.

Note that the basic simplicity of the apparatus allows you to invent your own variations. Thus, instead of paper balls, you can use rolled-up dollar bills. Different apparatus will suggest different patter and presentation. Note too that although a basically simple trick when you know the working, the cups and balls has stood the test of time as a true magical classic.

32. MOVIE STAR MAGIC

Movie stars and pop-music artists are always in the news. If you can tie them into a magic trick, the trick takes on an air of glamour. This routine, a favorite of Ben Christopher, is an excellent example of just such a trick.

The magician displays about a dozen slips of paper on which have been written the names of different movie stars. Half of the slips are given to the spectator. Each person holds his slips of paper behind his back and chooses one.

The magician and the spectator exchange their chosen slips. Each places the slip he holds into his packet, but reversed, so the writing side is up. Then each person brings his slips into view. The spectator's slip has the name of a female movie star. The performer's slip is seen to have the same name. Both the spectator and the magician have chosen the *same* female movie star!

The audience should be skeptical at this point. Certainly one of them will remark that perhaps all the slips contain the same name. All of the other slips are turned writing-side up and it is here that the second surprise happens. The slips do contain the same name, but the name is of a *male* movie star!

METHOD: Just the 12 slips of paper are used, and there are no gimmicks. The spectator actually has a free choice of any slip of paper. The ingenuity of the method lies in the handling.

On ten of the slips write the name of a male movie star. For this example we'll use the classic movie comedy figure Charlie Chaplin. Simply write Chaplin's name on ten of the slips. On the other two slips write the name of a female star. Here we'll use the name Greta Garbo.

Turn all of the slips so the writing side is down. Place the two Garbo slips on the table, one on top of the other. Then place the ten Chaplin slips on top of these. This is the only preparation.

To present the routine, hold the slips writing-side down. Explain that the slips contain the names of different movie stars. Deal off the top six and hand them to the spectator. Have him place them behind his back. The writing side of the slips is down. Place the other six slips behind your back, writing side down.

Request the spectator to remove any slip from the six he holds. You pretend to do likewise with your six slips, but really remove the bottom slip from the packet. This is a Garbo slip.

You and the spectator exchange slips. Tell him to place the

slip you just gave him behind his back, turn it writing side up, and insert it into the middle of his packet.

Pretend to do the same with the slip he gave you. Actually place it writing side down on top of your packet. Then remove the bottom slip from your packet (the other Garbo slip), turn it writing-side up, and insert it into your packet of slips.

Each of you brings your paper slips out, fans them and removes the face-up slip. The first surprise is that you both chose Garbo. But someone in the audience will always voice the suspicion that all the slips have Garbo written on them. This sets up the second surprise. Have the other slips turned over. They do indeed contain the same name, but it is a male movie star, in this case Chaplin.

When doing the trick be sure to use current stars as this adds to the audience interest. You can even start with 12 blank slips and have people call out the names of their favorite stars. Write the same male name on ten of the slips as you pretend to write the different names called out, then write the name of the same female star on the remaining two slips.

The trick stems from a two-deck card effect of Dr. Jaks. If 12 slips of paper are not readily available, or if you wish to do the trick with cards, use the Four of Heart and Four of Diamonds in place of the Garbo slips, and any ten black cards in place of the Chaplin slips. The setup and handling are the same. At the finish it is shown that you and the spectator each chose a red Four. Then comes the further surprise that you chose the only red cards in otherwise black packets.

33. HOCUS POCUS PUPPET

Children are fascinated with hand puppets and tend to relate to them as if they were real people. Puppet tricks tie in well with many of the tricks in this book because, although the tricks are self-working, it will appear as if the puppet makes the magic work.

Some magicians carry hand puppets with them if they know they are going to work for children, but I think it better to construct a puppet from the materials readily at hand. Not only is this more convenient for you, but it tends to squelch the idea that you use special apparatus to achieve your miracles.

A hand puppet that is extremely simple to make, but which looks authentic, is the one described here. Along with it I'll describe a trick that works very well with the puppet.

The only requirement is a pocket handkerchief or cloth table napkin. Tie a large but loose knot in one end. Slide your left index finger into the knot. Then extend your left palm so it is wide open, Figure 51. Your left thumb and middle finger will act as the puppet's arms.

FIG. 51.   FIG. 52.

Draw the handkerchief closed and hold it in place with the third and fourth fingers of your left hand. The result is the puppet shown in Figure 52. You can make the puppet with your hands lowered below the level of the tabletop, or, when you are familiar with the handling, with the handkerchief behind the back.

Bring the hand puppet into view, saying, "This is Tommy Turban. He speaks no English, but I can communicate with him." Turn your attention to the puppet. "I understand you do a few tricks?" Wiggle the left index finger and the puppet will appear to nod its head.

"And your specialty is tricks with fishes?" The puppet shakes its head "No." To this you say, "I meant dishes. You do tricks with dishes, right?" The puppet leans toward you and appears to whisper in your ear.

"Aha, tricks with dishes and glasses." Hold the dish in your right hand. The puppet picks up the glass and places it on the rim of the dish. When the puppet releases its grip on the glass, the glass mysteriously remains balanced on the edge of the dish. Actually, the glass rests secretly on the thumb as shown in Figure 53.

Fig. 53.

Allow the puppet to take a bow. Then the puppet grasps the glass and tips it up as if to take a drink from the glass. "His bedtime glass of milk," you explain. Place the dish on the table, remove the glass from the puppet's hand, let him take another bow, say, "He needs a rest after that balancing act," and place the puppet in your pocket.

All of this may seem matter-of-fact in print, but tricks with puppets have a charming quality that captivates children.

34. AN AMAZING APPLE

Although this trick has been known for many years, it is seldom seen, perhaps because the effect is not easy to appreciate from a printed description. It is a visual illusion and an astounding one at that. There are no gimmicks and it can be performed in the home or at a restaurant with borrowed props. The illusion is truly remarkable, but the reader must try it out to appreciate the visual effect that is created.

As the audience sees it, the magician, seated at the table, removes an apple from a bowl of fruit, studies it and says, "It has to be just ripe enough for this to work." As yet no one knows what it is that is supposed to work, so the others at the table will be curious.

The magician tosses the apple straight down at the floor. Instantly the apple hits the floor and bounces eight feet into the air! The magician replaces the apple and picks up a pear. He tosses it straight down, whereupon the pear bounces high into the air.

The trick can be done with any small object, even an egg or a dinner roll. In every case the object will not break when it hits the floor. Instead, it bounces high into the air and is then caught by the magician, who returns it to the table as if nothing out of the ordinary happened.

METHOD: As mentioned, there is no gimmick. The trick depends on a bit of eye-ear deception and coordination. The audience *sees* you toss the apple to the floor, *hears* it hit the floor and *sees* it bounce high into the air. It is between the seeing and the hearing that the deception occurs.

First, the others at the table should be seated across from you. To perform the trick, pull your chair out a bit so you are away from the table. Pick up an apple (or any piece of fruit) with your right hand. Turn your body slightly to the right.

Raise your right hand to about shoulder level and pretend to toss the apple against the floor. Actually the right hand moves swiftly down to a position below the tabletop and immediately your right foot taps against the floor, Figure 54.

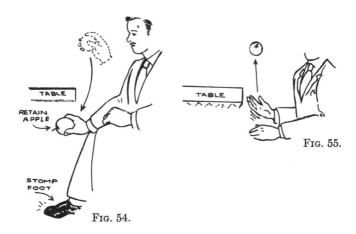

Fig. 54.

Fig. 55.

At the same time your right hand turns at the wrist so it is palm up. The fingers of your right hand then toss the apple into the air, Figure 55. This completes the illusion. The audience thinks you tossed an apple onto the floor and caused it to bounce ten feet into the air. But the apple never left your hand. It was merely brought below the level of the tabletop, then thrown into the air. Although this reads rather tame, the illusion, properly performed, is astonishing.

In practicing the effect there is one point that is important. Do not toss the apple down and then wait a split second before tapping the foot. This may seem the common sense thing to do because the apple should be allowed a split second to reach the floor, but in fact this detracts from the illusion. As soon as your right hand moves down below the level of the tabletop, your right foot taps.

The other point is that when your right hand is turned at the wrist and the upward-throwing motion made, make sure you do not inadvertenly raise your right hand above the level of the tabletop. The right arm remains stationary. The throwing action is accomplished by the fingers of your right hand only. As the apple begins its descent from the ceiling, it may be caught by either hand. The trick can be done with a dinner roll or other incongruous object.

35. THE APPLE MONSTER

This is the author's presentation of the above trick. The magician explains that there lives below the table a friendly monster who loves apples. He must be fed from time to time, though his owner has to be quick about it.

The magician is given an apple, which he shows all around. The apple is tossed down onto the floor. Immediately it flies up into the air, but a large bite has been taken out of it!

METHOD: Two apples are used. One apple has a large bite taken from it. This apple is in the left hand, which rests in the lap. The other apple is on the table at the start. Hand it to someone and ask him to polish it with a table napkin. The reason for this is to demonstrate that the apple is whole and ungimmicked.

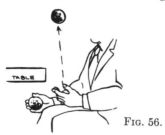

Fig. 56.

Take back the apple with the right hand. Pretend to toss it onto the floor. Actually you just bring your right hand sharply down and let it rest on your lap. At the same time your right foot taps against the floor, and then your left hand tosses its apple into the air, Figure 56.

Leave the good apple in your lap and catch the other apple with both hands. What the audience sees is that you tossed an apple to an unseen creature under the table. It took a bite and then tossed the apple back to you.

Since what is at work here is a switch done under the comedy guise of bouncing a normally unbounceable object onto the floor, it can be exploited in many ways. All that is required is a bit of practice, preferably before a mirror, to get the timing down.

36. THE GREAT BOTTLE MYSTERY

Make a hoop out of stiff paper and rest it on top of an empty bottle. Then balance a regular-size cigarette on top of the hoop. By striking the hoop, Figure 57, you cause the hoop to fly away and the cigarette to drop into the bottle. It looks easy enough but others who try it fail miserably.

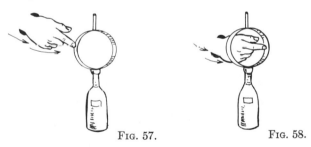

Fig. 57.   Fig. 58.

The secret depends on the way the hoop is struck. After you set up the apparatus, bring your forefinger near the side of the hoop, as if gauging the exact spot where you want to strike it.

This is in fact pure misdirection. If you hit the side of the hoop you cannot cause the cigarette to fall into the bottle. When you strike the hoop you must hit it at the inside, at a point indicated in Figure 58. Since your hand sweeps quickly as it strikes the hoop, the audience can't tell exactly where the hoop was struck. And anyone not knowing the secret is doomed to failure.

If no cigarette is available you can use any small object, such as a pea, a coin, or a small nail resting on its head. Balance the nail on top of the hoop, strike the hoop in the right place, and the nail will fall straight down into the bottle.

37. MYSTERY SPINNER

The magician remarks that eggs purchased in the northern hemisphere tend to spin on their side. Eggs purchased in the southern hemisphere spin on their end. But eggs purchased at the equator spin both ways.

The magician spins an egg on its side. Since it is an equatorial egg, it spins that way for a moment, then it flips up mysteriously and spins on end.

METHOD: The patter about the difference between northern and southern hemisphere eggs is pure bluff. Actually the real secret is that you must use a hardboiled egg. Leave the hardboiled egg in the refrigerator until you are ready to perform this trick.

Take the egg from the refrigerator. As you patter about northern hemisphere eggs, gently spin the egg on its side. When you patter about southern hemisphere eggs, spin the egg on end.

Now remark that eggs purchased at the equator spin both ways. "Since this is in fact an equatorial egg, I can show you what I mean." Give the egg a vigorous spin on its side. It will spin that way for a few moments, then it will mysteriously flip up on end and continue spinning.

The spinning trick works with many egg-shaped objects. Try it with wooden darning eggs or plastic egg-shaped containers.

38. STRONG MAN STUNT

This is strictly a show-off stunt. Roll a paper napkin diagonally from corner to corner to form a tight paper tube. Have a spectator grasp one end of the napkin in each hand and pull the napkin apart. Oddly enough, he will find it difficult or impossible to break the napkin. Yet when you try it, the napkin breaks easily.

METHOD: The secret is that while the spectator struggles to break the napkin, you secretly moisten your thumb and fingers. This is easily done by picking up a glass that contains a cold drink. Wet the fingers with the moisture that has condensed on the outside of the glass.

When you take the napkin from the spectator transfer the moisture to the center of the napkin. Grasp the napkin by the ends and pull. It will break easily.

39. CALCULATED CAPITAL

With computers taking over so many routine activities, it is not surprising that they might someday even replace road maps. If you want to know where you are, punch in the right information and the computer will pinpoint your location.

Fortunately this futuristic vision can be demonstrated right now and you don't need a computer. Any pocket calculator will do. The routine was suggested by Peter Alexis.

"By way of example," you say, "I'm thinking of a city in Idaho. It has a population of 30,000, the speed limit is 55, the highest mountain is 5,000 feet and a good steak dinner costs 53 dollars."

The spectator punches in 30,000, then adds to it each of the other numbers. The result he gets will be 35,108.

"And that tells you exactly where you are," you remark.

The spectator will not know what you're talking about. Have him turn the calculator upside down. When viewed upside down, most computer numbers look like letters. In this case 35,108 viewed upside down becomes BOISE.

40. BALLOON BURST

An inflated red balloon is placed inside an empty paper bag. The magician pushes a pin or needle into the side of the bag. There is a popping sound and it seems as if the balloon has burst. But when the balloon is removed from the paper bag, it hasn't burst, it has changed color and is now blue!

METHOD: Two balloons are used. Insert a blue balloon into a red balloon. Inflate the blue balloon and tie off the end. Then inflate the red balloon slightly so there is an air space between the two balloons, Figure 59. Tie off the end of the red balloon.

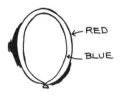

FIG. 59.

The basic idea is this. If you touch the point of a pin or needle to the red balloon it will burst, leaving you with the inflated blue balloon. Done this way the change is visible and instantaneous. There is a slight problem though in that the pieces of the burst red balloon aren't always completely concealed from sight. Thus although the red balloon bursts, it might leave traces of itself behind.

The alternative is to insert the inflated red balloon into a paper bag that has previously been shown empty. Insert the pin into the paper bag just enough to burst the red balloon. Then reach into the bag, do a double take as if surprised that the balloon is still there, then remove it and show that it has changed color. Crumple up the bag (indirectly proving it empty) and toss it aside.

A double color change can be brought about by inserting a yellow balloon inside a red balloon and these inside a blue balloon. Inflate and tie off the balloons as described above. Puncture the blue balloon and it changes to red. Puncture the red balloon and it changes to yellow. When setting up the trick make sure the outer balloon is darker than the inside one. This way the presence of the inside balloon is concealed from the audience's view.

Another approach is to insert two small blue balloons inside a large blue balloon. Inflate and tie off the two small balloons. Then inflate the large blue balloon slightly, creating the required airspace. When the large blue ballon is burst with a needle, it changes instantly into two small inflated blue balloons. It is a startling visual transformation which can be done in plain sight.

41. PUNCTURE PROOF

It is possible to push a straight pin or safety pin right through an inflated balloon without bursting the balloon. It is done in front of the audience and looks extremely strange as it is against all expectations to see a needle enter a balloon *without* bursting it.

Inflate a balloon and tie off the end. Then place a small piece of clear mending tape on one side of the balloon, Figure 60. The tape can't be seen by the audience if it is at the side of the

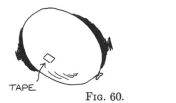

TAPE

FIG. 60.

FIG. 61.

balloon and the balloon is displayed between the hands, with the hands covering the tape.

Hold the balloon with one hand, the straight pin or safety pin with the other. Slowly push it in toward the center of the balloon, but make sure it punctures the balloon where the tape is, Figure 61. The tape acts as a self-seal and keeps the balloon from bursting.

Another approach is to place a spot of rubber cement on one side of the balloon and push the needle through the treated spot. If you use this approach, set it up just before doing the trick. The reason is that the rubber cement contains a chemical that tends to dissolve the material of the balloon.

42. AN AIRTIGHT CASE

The most recent method of piercing a balloon without causing it to burst is one which uses no gimmick, not even tape. It is based on an idea that appeared in a magician's journal. Inflate a balloon about three-quarters of the way and tie off the end. If you examine the balloon you will find a spot of thick rubber at the top and another near the neck. If you now insert a sharp knitting needle or skewer into the top and out the bottom, Figure 62, piercing the balloon through the thick spots, it will not burst.

FIG. 62.

Withdraw the needle and quickly burst the balloon by piercing it at some other spot. The reason for doing this rather quickly is to cover the fact that although the balloon doesn't burst in Figure 62, it does lose air, so you should puncture it before it deflates.

This version of the Needle Thru Balloon can also be done with a needle that is threaded with bright (but thin) ribbon. The sight of a needle and a ribbon going straight through the balloon is quite amazing to the audience.

43. LOOPS ENTWINED

The trick here is to cause two unprepared pieces of rope or string to become linked together. It is Jack Avis's fine handling of a trick that appeared in a magical journal called *The Phoenix,* and it is one of the best.

As the audience sees it, two loops of rope are placed on the table and partially covered with a handkerchief as shown in Figure 63. Note that the ends of the ropes are in view at all times.

The magician places his hands under the handkerchief, makes an adjustment, and then causes the two loops to become intertwined. Immediately all apparatus may be left with the audience.

METHOD: If possible secure two lengths of cotton rope. This type of rope is usually available from hardware stores. Ribbon or string can also be used, but rope is more visible. Each piece of rope or cord should measure about four feet in length. An opaque handkerchief or scarf is the only other requirement.

Place the two ropes on the tabletop so that each forms a U. Cover them with a handkerchief, Figure 63. Call attention to the fact that the ends of the ropes always remain in view. This

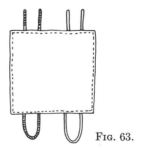

Fig. 63.

is true but misleading as there is a bit of misdirection on this point late in the trick.

Remark that you will try to cause the two loops to become

FIG. 64.

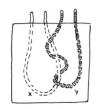

FIG. 65.

linked. Place your hands under the handkerchief. When you do, bring one rope over the other rope, Figure 64, then twist them as shown in Figure 65.

Grasp the left rope at "x" and the right rope at "y" and slide the loops out into view, Figure 66. The audience sees the impossible; the two solid ropes have become linked.

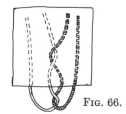

FIG. 66.

FIG. 67.

Now grasp the ropes and the handkerchief and raise them off the table, Figure 67. This is the subtle angle because behind the handkerchief the ends of the ropes disentangle themselves. Even if they don't, a slight shake with the hands will cause the ends to disentangle.

All that remains is to drop the handkerchief to the table. You are left with two linked ropes in the hands and no clue as to how the mystery was accomplished.

In the illustrations one rope is shown shaded for purposes of clarity. But in performance you can use ropes of different color. This adds eye appeal to the trick and in no way interferes with the method.

PSYCHIC TRICKS

Psychic and mind-reading tricks are among the most impressive you can do because they are accepted as real magic by almost everyone. The power of the mind is a subject of endless fascination. Although the tricks in this chapter depend on simple secrets, treat them seriously when presenting them because laymen are enormously impressed by demonstrations of mental prowess.

44. THE MIND DOWSER

Most people have heard of individuals who have the ability to dowse for water using a device known as a dowsing rod. Using common props you can set up an experiment where you dowse for thoughts.

Balance a strip of paper on a nickel as shown in Figure 68. Hand a spectator two inexpensive ballpoint pens. Tell him to rub them on his jacket sleeve or trouser leg, then to take one in each hand.

Fig. 68.

Have him hold the pens on either side of the paper, Figure 69, and draw them closer and closer to the paper. Although the pens are an equal distance on either side of the paper, in time the paper will slowly pivot either to the right or to the left. It is a strange sight.

Fɪɢ. 69.

If the paper pivots to the left, tell the spectator it indicates the left side of his brain is more active than the right side, indicating that he is a logical person who is good at figuring out problems.

If the paper pivots to the right, tell the spectator it indicates the right side of his brain is more active than the left, indicating that he is probably a creative individual who likes music and other forms of self-expression.

METHOD: When he rubs the pens against his jacket sleeve, the spectator charges the pens with static electricity. The spectator is likely to guess this anyway, but there still remains the fact that the paper 'will be attracted more to one pen than the other, even though the pens are equally charged.

When the pens are placed on either side of the paper, one pen will be fractionally closer to the paper than the other pen, so the paper will pivot toward the nearer pen.

The left-brain/right-brain interpretation you give is pure bluff. But since either statement flatters the spectator, he must agree you are correct. The important point though is that this simple experiment nicely sets up the following trick.

45. LEFT-HANDED THOUGHTS

Ask the spectator if he is right-handed or left-handed. Whatever his reply, act as if this information is important. Give him a penny and a nickel. While you turn your back, ask him to place one coin in each hand.

Face the spectator again. Ask him to multiply the value of the coin in his left hand by 12. Then have him multiply the value of the coin in his right hand by 14. When he has done this, ask him to merely think of the total of the two numbers.

Without asking a question, you immediately announce the total. The trick can be repeated with another spectator, and it can even be done over the telephone.

METHOD: This is the author's variation of a trick devised by Royal Heath. The secret is based on the fact that it will take the spectator longer to perform one of the multiplications than the other. Thus, if he has the penny in the left hand and you tell him to multiply the value of that coin by 12, he will *immediately* announce that he has the total. But if he has the nickel in his left hand, it will take him a few seconds to perform the multiplication.

So, if he hesitates when he performs the multiplication with the left-hand coin, the grand total will be 74. If he hesitates when performing the multiplication with the right-hand coin, the total is 82.

Since it is the hesitation you note, and nothing else, you can be blindfolded, in the next room, or even in the next town performing the trick by telephone. Do *not* tell the spectator which coin is in which hand because that is a direct tip-off to the method. Focus attention on the total of the two numbers and you will baffle even experts.

46. THE PSYCHIC MOTOR

The curious device described here has been around in one form or another for more than a century, yet the exact means by which it works is not clearly known, nor has the real secret of controlling its movement ever been revealed in print. To construct the motor, insert a needle into a cork. Take a square of paper measuring about 4 inches on a side and draw the diagonals to find the center. Bend two opposite corners of the paper over, one up and the other down. Then balance the paper on the needle, Figure 70.

Fig. 70.

Place a cupped hand near the paper. Nothing will happen at first, but then the paper will begin to spin. It may seem that heat from the hand or air currents are responsible for the spinning paper, but the actual mechanism is still something of a mystery.

To use the Psychic Motor in the context of a trick, draw an arrow on the paper before balancing it on the point of the needle. Then ask everyone present to concentrate on something he wishes will come true. Place your hand near the side of the Psychic Motor. It will spin for a while and then slow down and stop. The arrow will point to the person whose wish is about to come true.

METHOD: First it should be noted that there will be times when the Psychic Motor spins rapidly, other times it will reverse direction, and still other times when it will slow down, then speed up again, then stop. Since you want a controlled result, an additional ingredient is needed, and this is where the real secret comes into play.

If the motor refuses to spin, or if you want it to stop after it has spun a while, gently breathe in the direction of the paper. Do not purse the lips because this is a giveaway. All you want to do is disturb the air a small amount. The paper is delicately balanced, and any small disturbance set up by air currents will be more than enough to cause it to respond.

It requires a few minutes practice to develop the knack of controlling the spin, but it is worth it. In time you will be able to cause the Psychic Motor to stop with the arrow pointing at any desired spectator.

47. UNLISTED NUMBERS

Two-person telepathy involves a sender and a receiver, that is, someone to transmit thoughts and someone able to receive them. The following is an excellent test of two-person mind-reading.

The medium goes into an adjoining room and the door is closed behind her. The mentalist asks for a credit card or social-security card belonging to a man and one belonging to a woman. They are placed on the table before him.

A spectator will act as spokesman for the mentalist. This means that the mentalist will not speak throughout the test.

The two credit cards are placed on the table in front of the mentalist. The spectator indicates one of the cards. It can be the card belonging to the man or the card belonging to the woman. The mentalist places the chosen credit card behind his back.

He nods his head to indicate that he is beginning to concentrate. The spectator signals the medium by saying, "Begin." This is her signal to begin concentrating too.

When the mentalist thinks he has a clear mental image of the credit card, he nods his head again. The spectator signals the medium by saying, "Stop."

With no further communication between the medium and any other person, she reveals whether the chosen credit card belonged to a man or to a woman.

True, she could simply guess and would have an even-money chance of guessing correctly. But the test is repeated three or four more times, and each time the medium correctly guesses whether the chosen card belongs to a man or a woman.

For the startling conclusion, the mentalist hands one of the credit cards to the spectator, who in turn takes it into the next room to the medium. Concentrating for a few seconds, she proceeds to name four or five consecutive digits on the *other* credit card, the one she never saw!

METHOD: Oddly enough, the key to the first part of the trick depends on a quite unlikely method, the pulse beat. You will have to time this for yourself, but on the average, the pulse beats about six times every five seconds.

When you place the chosen credit card behind your back, secretly place your hand on your pulse. If the card given to you belongs to a man, nod your head so that the spectator says, "Begin," to the medium. Actually this is a signal to her to look at her watch and begin counting the seconds.

Wait six pulse beats, then nod again. The spectator says, "Stop." The medium merely notes that about five seconds elapsed on her watch and concludes that the chosen credit card belongs to a man.

If the chosen credit card belongs to a woman, wait about ten pulse beats. The medium in the next room, consulting her watch, sees that about ten seconds elapsed between the time she heard "Begin" and "Stop," so she concludes that the chosen credit card belongs to a woman.

After you perform the test the first time, people will naturally think the medium merely guessed. They will demand that you repeat the trick. Allow yourself to be talked into doing the trick again. The third or fourth time you do the trick you set things up for the grand climax. When a credit card is handed to you behind your back, go through the usual business with the pulse to code the right information to the medium. But pretend to have trouble and ask to repeat the trick. Under your belt or in your jacket sleeve tucked under your watch, is a pencil stub. Take it with the right hand and on the back of the card you hold, jot down four or five consecutive digits of the credit card still on the table. Make sure you use a pencil that will write on plastic. Your writing is done on the back of the credit card you hold. You can add the initials of the owner of the credit card on the table.

Proceed with the test described above. That is, once you've jotted down as much information as you can on the back of the credit card you hold behind your back, nod your head, signaling to the spectator that he is to say "Begin." Wait the appropriate number of pulse beats, then nod so that the spectator will say "Stop." The medium in the next room then announces whether the card in your hand belongs to a man or a women.

The card with the secret writing on the back is then handed to the spectator. Ask him to take it in to the medium. She is then left alone in the room for a few seconds.

When she is alone the medium turns over the card, memorizes the data you've jotted down on the back of the card, then wipes the pencil jottings off. She then proceeds to reveal four or five consecutive digits on the *other* card. It is a very strong finish to the trick.

48. RIGHT ON TIME

Tell someone you have a mental clock which registers any interval of time up to a minute. To demonstrate, have someone call out an interval. Say someone calls out an interval of 20 seconds. Ask him to consult his watch. You say, "Go," and then a bit later say "Stop." You have said "Stop" exactly 20 seconds after you said "Go." The trick may of course be repeated.

METHOD: The secret is the same as in the previous trick. You use your pulse beat to accurately estimate the passage of any number of seconds up to a minute. The trick can be done with the hands behind the back where you feel the pulse directly, but there is another method that is not at all well known.

There is also a pulse beat at the temple, that is, at the side of the forehead. It you touch the temple lightly with the fingertips you can feel the pulse. Note and remember how many pulse beats there are for intervals of 15, 30, 45 and 60 seconds. The intervals in between can be estimated to a reasonable degree of accuracy.

The subtle angle here is that when you touch the fingertips to the temple and close the eyes, it appears exactly as if you are concentrating. No one except a doctor will realize that you are telling time by your own pulsebeat.

49. THE MIND TRANSMITTER

This is another two-person test which looks like genuine telepathy but is really based on simple trickery. While the medium is in another room, the mentalist hands a pen and a pad to a spectator and asks him to draw a circle in the center of the pad. He then removes any coin from his pocket, places it in the circle for a moment, and then returns the coin to his pocket. Say the coin was a dime.

Tearing off the top sheet of the pad, the spectator takes it and the pen to the medium. She concentrates for a moment, then writes in the circle the value of the chosen coin. In our example she would write "10¢."

The trick can be repeated and the medium always correctly guesses the value of the chosen coin. At times she can even name the *date* on the chosen coin!

METHOD: A code is used, but it rests on a seemingly innocent object, the pen. The pen is of the inexpensive plastic type with a cap. Examine any such pen and you will find the manufacturer's name written on the pen. The code depends on how the cap is placed on the pen in relation to the manufacturer's name.

If you place the cap on the pen so that the clip points directly at the name, Figure 71, you signal that the chosen coin is a penny. With the pen held upright, if the clip on cap lies to the

FIG. 71.

left of the name, the spectator chose a nickel, and if it lies to the right of the name, the chosen coin was a dime. If the clip lies opposite the name, the chosen coin was a quarter.

To present the routine, remove the cap from the pen and draw a large circle on the top sheet of the pad. Ask a spectator to remove any coin from his pocket. As soon as you see the coin, replace the cap on the pen in the appropriate way. As you do this, tell the spectator to place the coin inside the circle, leave it there a second and then return it to his pocket.

He tears off the top sheet of the pad and takes this, plus the pen, to the medium. Glancing at the way the cap has been placed on the pen, the medium immediately knows the chosen coin.

As to guessing the date on a coin, you and the medium agree that the first time she will be asked to guess the date on a coin, it will be a 1980 coin. The second time, it will be a 1975 coin, the next time a 1977 coin, and so on in some order agreed upon by you and the medium. In other words, you wait until a coin bearing the first agreed upon date is used before you ask the medium for the date on the coin.

When you see that a spectator has placed a 1980 coin on the paper, tell him to remove the coin but to keep it in his clenched fist. Then the medium guesses the value of the coin and goes on to reveal the date. The next time she is asked to guess the date on a coin, it will be a 1975 coin. The next time it will be a 1977 coin, and so on, in the sequence you and she have agreed on.

If the pen cap has a round end without a clip, or if there is no manufacturer's name on the pen, use small scratch marks made with a sharp pin or knife. The relative position of the scratch marks then key the value of the chosen coin.

50. CLOCKS

A spectator sets the hands of his watch at any hour. He gives you the watch behind your back. Taking off your watch, and with both watches always behind the back, you proceed to set the hands of your watch at the *same* hour as the spectator's watch. There are no gimmicks.

METHOD: The trick depends on nerve and self-confidence because it is basically a swindle. First, have the hands of your watch set at exactly 12 o'clock. Now, while your back is turned, ask a spectator to set the hands of his watch at any hour. He then gives you his watch behind your back.

Turn so you face the audience. As soon as you do, slip the spectator's watch onto your right wrist. Walk over to a spectator who is to one side. Tell him you are having trouble removing your watch. Extend your right hand and ask him to slip your watch off. Of course this is the *spectator's* watch, not yours, and as soon as you extend your hand, you glimpse the setting on the watch. Thank the spectator and take the watch behind your back.

This much of the method is the author's. But now there is the problem of setting the magician's watch to match the spectator's, and for this we turn to an ingenious idea of Peter Mac-Donald's. Slip your watch off your wrist and hold the watch in your left hand.

Pull the winding stem out with your right hand. While your right hand holds the winding stem stationary, your left hand revolves the watch one full turn, Figure 72. This will advance the

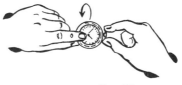

Fig. 72.

hands one full hour. Give the watch enough full turns to insure that the setting on your watch matches the spectator's. For example, if the spectator's watch is set at five o'clock, give your watch five full turns. This will advance the hands on your watch to match the setting on the spectator's watch. It may not match the setting exactly, but it will be close enough to impress the audience.

51. THE EIGHT-OBJECT TEST

Eight ordinary objects are placed in an empty box. The spectator looks down into the box and mentally decides on one object. The mentalist then removes objects from the box at random, then replaces them in the box.

For each object removed and replaced, the spectator mentally spells the name of his chosen object, one letter at a time. When he gets to the last letter, he calls stop. The object held by the mentalist in his hand at that point is the chosen object. The mentalist never knows the identity of the chosen object until the spectator calls stop, yet the mentalist is always correct. The trick may be repeated without fear of detection.

METHOD: The objects you use are a key, a book, a watch, a pencil, a quarter, an envelope, a toothpick and a half-dollar. Note that most of the objects are small enough to be concealed when held in the closed hand. Thus, when you remove your hand from the box each time, the spectator knows the hand contains an object, but he doesn't know the identity of the object.

Each time you lift an object from the box, the spectator mentally spells one letter in the name of his thought-of object. The first two objects you lift from the box are any two random objects. But thereafter you lift objects in the exact order given above. When the spectator gets to the last letter in his mental spell, he calls stop. Open your hand and it will contain the thought-of object.

The trick works because the name of each of the objects is spelled with one more letter than the previous object.

52. BEHIND CLOSED DOORS

A spectator goes into another room with pad and pencil. On your instruction he draws any simple geometric figure on the paper, and then draws another geometric symbol inside that. He is asked to concentrate on what he has written. When he feels that he has a clear mental image of the two symbols, he says he is ready.

The mentalist writes something on a large pad. When the spectator returns, his pictures are compared to the mentalist's and they are the same.

METHOD: The truth is that in *most* cases the symbols will match. Occasionally you will get one right and one wrong. On rare occasions you will get both wrong, but most of the time you will be right. Further, there is a way to narrow the chances of failure virtually to the vanishing point.

The trick depends on a little known psychic secret. Asked to draw a simple geometric symbol, most people will choose either a circle or a triangle. If they draw a circle, and then are asked to draw another simple symbol inside that, they will almost always draw a triangle. There may be some subconscious prodding involved here because the simplest geometric symbols are the circle and the triangle. In any event, most of the time the spectator will draw one of these symbols and then will draw the other inside it.

While the spectator is outside the room drawing the chosen symbols, you need merely draw a circle with a triangle inside it. Draw the symbols on a large pad for maximum visibility. If you draw the triangle inside the circle and the spectator draws a circle inside a triangle, the test can still be considered a success. If the spectator draws, say, a square inside a circle, you have still gotten one symbol right, so the test is still impressive.

If you want to really increase your chances to a near-certain 100 percent correct match, there is an easy way to do it. Give pads and pencils to two spectators. Direct them to opposite corners of the room to do their writing. When they return and compare their results with yours, it is almost certain that at least one spectator will have drawn a triangle and the other a circle. Remark that you picked up the strongest thought from each spectator to make your drawing.

53. THE BORGIA CUP

The closing trick in this chapter is a splendid combination of an effect of Oscar Weigle's and a method of Bob Hummer's. The patter centers around the fact that the Borgias were known to kill their enemies by poisoning the wine served up to their victims during dinner. When you were a guest at the Borgia house it payed to know from which cup you drank.

To enact the drama the magician uses three cups. While his back is turned or he is out of the room, a spectator hides a "poison" pill under one cup. The cups are mixed and the mentalist returns. Without asking a question he reveals which cup contains the poison.

METHOD: The "poison" pill can be a vitamin capsule, an aspirin tablet or even a slip of paper with the word "Poison" written on it. Three teacups or coffee containers are also used.

The method depends on the fact that one cup will invariably have a slight imperfection which you can spot, allowing you to later identify that cup. Plastic coffee containers have knicks in them, and if they don't, you can easily put one on with a fingernail. The important point is that you must be able to positively identify one particular cup.

Patter about the Borgia family's unique interest in poison. As you patter, place the three cups mouth-down on the table. Arrange things so that the cup with the secret mark is at the far left of the row. Place the poison capsule in front of the cups.

While you turn your back, have a spectator silently lift any cup and place the poison capsule under that cup. He then switches the position of the two cups that do *not* contain the poison. The switch is done silently by sliding the cups on the table, not by lifting them. This way there is less chance of the marked cup dropping or having its position altered so that you can no longer see the mark.

Turn around and face the spectator. Remark that you are going to try to guess which two cups do not contain the poison, adding, "If we were back in the time of the Borgias, and I guessed wrong, the mistake would be fatal." Glance at the three cups as you talk.

If the marked cup is in its original position at the far left, the poison is under that cup. If the marked cup is in the middle, the poison is under the cup at the far right. And if the marked cup is at the far right, the poison is under the middle cup.

As soon as you know which cup contains the poison, begin to act as if you are unsure. Start to reach for a cup, hesitate, change your mind, move on to another cup, again hesitate, and so on. Build up audience expectation, finally turn one cup over. Act relieved that it doesn't contain the poison, then build tension again as you try to decide which of the remaining cups is safe to turn over. Finally turn over the cup that doesn't contain the poison, leaving just the poison cup on the table.

With the proper build up this is a masterpiece of deception.

ELASTIC ILLUSIONS

As in the chapter on match tricks, the tricks in this chapter have been arranged to form a miniature magic act. The only major item of apparatus is a rubber band, yet, as you will discover, there is a truly amzing range of tricks and puzzles which can be performed with this simple prop.

54. TWISTER

The performer puts a twist in a rubber band and then hands the twisted band to a spectator. The spectator grasps a strand of the rubber band in each hand and is requested to untwist the band without letting go of it.

Although the task seems childishly easy, the spectator is unable to untwist the band. The magician takes it back and slowly untwists it. Even if the effect is repeated, the spectator finds it impossible to untwist the band.

METHOD: This excellent close-up mystery was invented by Alex Elmsley. to perform it, take a large rubber band and hold it as shown in Figure 73. By moving or sliding the right thumb and first finger in the direction indicated by the arrows twice, you will impart two twists to the band as shown in Figure 74.

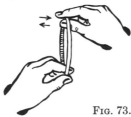

FIG. 73.

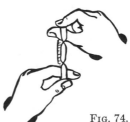

FIG. 74.

With the rubber band in this condition, have a spectator grasp it as shown in Figure 75. Explain to him that the object of the puzzle is to remove the twists from the band without chang-

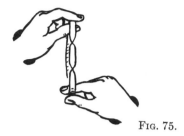

Fig. 75.

ing his grip on the ends of the band or letting go of either end. Other than this, he can change the position of his hands any way he desires to remove the twists from the band.

In time the spectator will find it impossible to untwist the band. When he gives up, take the band back from him, holding it exactly as in Figure 74. Then slowly move the hands to the position of Figure 76. Strangely enough, the twists in the band will slowly vanish as you do this.

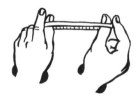

Fig. 76.

55. TALE TWISTER

This is a variation of Elmsley's stunt. In this version the hands never contact the rubber band. Besides the rubber band you will need two pens or pencils which have clips.

Slide the rubber bands under the clips and hold the two pens as shown in Figure 77. Slowly raise the left hand pen and lower the right hand pen to the position shown in Figure 78.

Now have the spectator grasp the pens as indicated in Figure 79. Tell him that the object is to untwist the rubber band. The

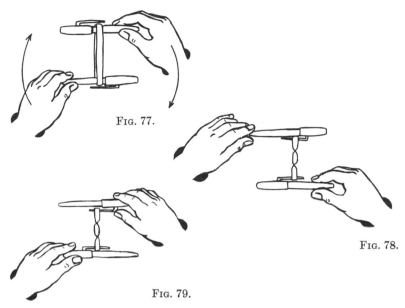

Fig. 77.

Fig. 78.

Fig. 79.

rubber band must remain in the clips and can't be rotated or twisted within the clips. To insure this, at the start you can tape the rubber band in place so it is permanently fastened to the pens in Figure 77.

Although the spectator has been given a simple task, he will find it impossible to untwist the rubber bands. When he gives up, take back the apparatus. Simply reverse the action of the arrows in Figure 77 and you will be back at the starting position. In the process the twists in the rubber band will have magically vanished.

Knowing how the trick works, the reader may now try to figure out why it works.

56. SLIPPERY SHEARS

Loop a rubber band over an open pair of scissors and have the spectator grip the handles as shown in Figure 80. Then toss a handkerchief over the apparatus. You reach under the handkerchief, make a small adjustment, and then remove the handkerchief. The rubber band is now looped around the shears as shown by the dotted lines in Figure 80.

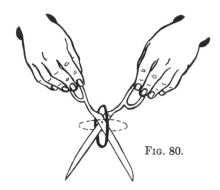

FIG. 80.

METHOD: An extra rubber band is concealed in the jacket sleeve. Under cover of the handkerchief, cut the first rubber band loose by moving it against the cutting edge of the scissors until it has a nick in it. Then it can be broken silently between the fingers and tossed into the jacket sleeve.

Remove the other rubber band from the jacket sleeve and loop it over the scissors as shown by the dotted line in Figure 80. Since all this takes place while the spectator firmly holds the handles of the scissors, the effect appears impossible.

To divert attention away from the rubber band, remark that you have a magical pair of shears given to you by a mystic. By focusing attention on the scissors, you direct attention away from the rubber band and therefore away from the method.

57. BET A BAND

Originally a puzzle, this stunt with a rubber band is ideal as a betting wager. Place a rubber band on the first finger, Figure 81. With your right hand grasp the band and bring it around the middle finger as shown in Figure 82. Then hook it back over the first finger, Figure 83. The situation must be exactly as depicted in Figure 83 for the stunt to work.

FIG. 81.

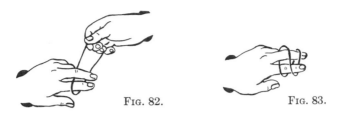

FIG. 82. FIG. 83.

Ask a spectator to grasp your first finger. As soon as he does, bend the middle finger, and with the aid of the left thumb if necessary, slide the band free of the first finger. The rubber band will end up hooked on the middle finger as shown in Figure 84.

SPECTATOR'S HAND

FIG. 84.

This is the original form of the puzzle. To turn it into a bet, explain to the spectator that the rubber band will always end up hooked on either the first finger or the second finger. Set up the rubber band as in Figure 83. The spectator grasps either finger, betting that the rubber band will end up on that finger. Every time he is wrong.

If he grasps the first finger, proceed as above. If he grasps the second finger, simply slide the rubber band free of that finger, allowing it to hook onto the first finger. Thus, either way, he loses.

58. THE JUMPING RUBBER BAND

Introduced near the turn of the century by Stanley Collins, the jumping rubber band has become a classic of close-up magic. Some of the best versions of this fine trick are discussed here.

The basic effect is that an ordinary rubber band is looped around the first and second fingers. Instantly it jumps to a position around the third and fourth fingers.

METHOD: Place the rubber band over the first and second fingers of your right hand, as shown in Figure 85. Your left hand does not let go of the rubber band. Instead, as the fingers of the right hand curl in to make a fist, loop the band over the tips of all four fingers as shown in Figure 86.

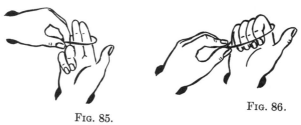

FIG. 85.

FIG. 86.

Now if you suddenly extend all four fingers, the rubber band will jump to a position over the third and fourth fingers as shown in Figure 87.

FIG. 87.

Harlan Tarbell suggested placing a rubber band over the first and second fingers, but then twisting a second rubber band over all four fingertips as shown in Figure 88. The audience thinks

FIG. 88.

that the first band is trapped by the second, but if you perform the handling outlined above, the first rubber band will still jump when the fingers are extended.

59. DOUBLE JUMP

In this routine two rubber bands change places visibly. Place a rubber band over the first and second fingers, and a rubber band of a different color over the third and fourth fingers, Figure 89. As you close the right hand into a fist, draw the first

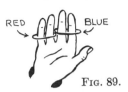

RED   BLUE

FIG. 89.

rubber band over the fintertips as explained above. Then draw the second rubber band over the fingertips. Keep the palm of your right hand toward you as you do this. The audience may be aware that you are doing something, but they do not know what.

Have them note the color of the rubber band on the right. Say it is red. Extend all four fingers and the red rubber band will now be on the left. The two rubber bands change places instantly. The double jump was suggested by Fred Furman.

60. FLYING CLIPPER

Bruce Elliott's version of the jumping rubber band is perhaps the most magical. Oddly enough it is not the rubber band which jumps, but a paper clip. Begin by fastening a paper clip to a rubber band. Then place the rubber band over the first and second fingers of your right hand. Place a second rubber band of the same color over the third and fourth fingers.

Curl the fingers into a fist. As you do, loop the first band over all four fingers as in Figure 86. Then loop the second band over all four fingers. Call attention to the position of the paper clip, Figure 90. If you now extend all four fingers, it appears as if the paper clip jumped to the other rubber band.

FIG. 90.

Actually the rubber bands changed places as before, but since they are the same color, no one notices that they've changed places. Thus the illusion you create is that the paper clip jumped from one band to the other.

61. A QUICK GETAWAY

The effect is that a rubber band penetrates a pencil while the spectator holds both ends of the pencil. The routine is based on a very fine trick of Ken Beale's.

METHOD: You will need a rubber band, a pencil and a file card or business card. A playing card may also be used.

Loop the rubber band over the file card as shown in Figure 91. Now as the left hand reaches into the pocket for the pencil, secretly slide the rubber band up past the center of the card with the right thumb as shown in Figure 92. This is done behind the card so the audience is unaware of the secret action.

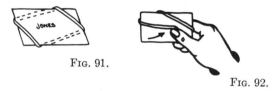

Fig. 91.

Fig. 92.

Push the pencil through the center of the card. It appears as if the pencil traps the rubber band as well, Figure 93, but because of the secret handling, the rubber band is already free of the pencil.

PENCIL IS
PUSHED
THRU CENTER OF CARD.

Fig. 93.

Have the spectator hold the ends of the pencil. Say you will attempt to free the rubber band from the business card without tearing the card. Pretend to fumble with the card. Finally pull the rubber band off the card. Act surprised that the rubber band not only came free of the card and that it came free of the pencil as well.

62. STRANGE INTERLUDE

The last trick in this chapter is also the newest in the literature. The invention of Neal Thomas, it begins as a simple puzzle but ends rather strangely as two rubber bands become one.

The magician displays two small rubber bands, saying that he would like to demonstrate a puzzle. He places the two bands below the level of the tabletop, arranges them a certain way, and then brings the hands up into view. The situation is as shown in Figure 94, with the rubber bands at right angles to one another.

Fig. 94.

The rubber bands are tossed to the spectator. Of course he has no trouble duplicating the situation of Figure 94. Anyone can do it. After the spectator has succeeded, the magician, acting puzzled, says, "I think there's an element missing. Here, let me show you again."

Taking back the two rubber bands, the magician again forms the configuration of Figure 94. The no-doubt exasperated spectator will insist that it's a childishly simple puzzle and that he got it right the first time. But when he takes the two rubber bands from the magician, he is surprised to find that they have changed to a single large band!

METHOD: The reader should have no trouble forming the configuration of Figure 94 with two small bands. The real secret to this trick is forming the same configuration with a single large band.

Three rubber bands are needed for the routine. Two are small. The third band is twice the size of either of the other two. The large band is in the lap at the start of the trick. To begin the routine, form the configuration of Figure 94 with the two small bands. Challenge the spectator to duplicate it. Of course he does.

Take back the two bands. Lower your hands into your lap. Say, "I don't think you quite got it. Let me show you again."

Drop the two small bands into your lap and grasp the large rubber band. Place the large band on your right forefinger, Figure 95, grasp end *A* with the left hand and give the rubber band a twist in the direction of the arrow.

FIG. 95.

The situation now is shown in Figure 96. Give the band another twist in the direction of the arrow in Figure 96. The result is shown in Figure 97. Slip your right middle finger through loop *X*. You've now reached the situation of Figure 98.

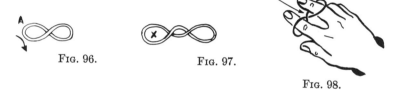

FIG. 96.   FIG. 97.

FIG. 98.

Grasp the strand indicated by the arrow in Figure 98 and pull it upward. The result is the required configuration of Figure 94. The entire sequence from Figure 95 to Figure 98 is accomplished in about two seconds.

Bring the rubber band up into view again. It appears as if you have two small rubber bands at right angles to one another. Say to the spectator, "*This* is how it should look."

He'll fall for the bait. Thinking you have just two small rubber bands, he will grab for them and will be amazed to discover that they have changed into one large band. It is a surprising outcome.

HANKY PANKY

All of the tricks in this chapter use an ordinary cotton or linen handkerchief as the major item of apparatus. A cloth table napkin may also be used. Although a handkerchief folds up into a small package and can easily be carried in the pocket, in its unfolded state it is a large piece of apparatus, easily visible even from the platform or stage.

The chapter opens with some basic handkerchief knots, then moves on to penetration effects and closes with a spectacular routine built around a special handkerchief fold.

63. NOT A KNOT

The magician appears to tie a secure knot in a handkerchief, yet the knot instantly disappears. There are many ways of accomplishing this effect. One of the most convincing is the following method.

METHOD: Clip the end of a handkerchief between the first and second fingers of your left hand. Then loop the handkerchief around the back of the left hand and across the palm as shown in Figure 99.

FIG. 99.

Now place end *B* through the loop, forming the apparent knot of Figure 100.

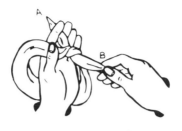

FIG. 100.

Do not let go of end B with the right hand. As you give the knotted handkerchief to the spectator behind his back, slip end A out with your left hand. This has the effect of dissolving the knot. The spectator grasps end B behind his back, thinking that the handkerchief is still knotted. When he removes the handkerchief, the knot has vanished.

64. THE APPEARING KNOT

This effect is the opposite of "Not a Knot." Here you hand a spectator an ordinary handkerchief behind his back. You snap your fingers. When he removes the handkerchief, a knot has mysteriously formed in the center.

METHOD: Begin by placing a handkerchief over the hand as shown in Figure 101. Note that end B hangs down lower than end A. Note too that end B is clipped between the third and fourth fingers.

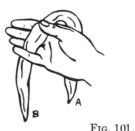

FIG. 101.

The right hand turns palm down. In the same motion end A is clipped between the first and second fingers, Figure 102. Release the third and fourth finger's grip on end B.

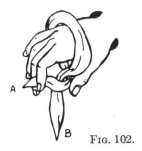

Fɪɢ. 102.

With a sharp downward movement of your right hand, shake the handkerchief off your right wrist. The result is that a knot is tied in the center of the handkerchief, Figure 103. With just a

Fɪɢ. 103.

bit of practice the one-hand knot can be formed instantly. If you have trouble getting the handkerchief to slide off your hand, twist it rope fashion before placing it on your hand in Figure 101. If the knot is formed in view of the audience, it happens so quickly that it will appear as if you shook the handkerchief and a knot mysteriously formed in the center.

65. TRANSPOSITION

"Not a Knot" and "The Appearing Knot" can be routined together to produce an effect where a knot travels from one handkerchief to another. Required are two handkerchiefs and two spectators. Display one handkerchief, tie a knot in it and give it to a spectator to hold behind his back. Actually you go through the procedure described in "Not a Knot," so that when the knotted handkerchief is given to the spectator behind his back, the knot dissolves.

Now display another handkerchief and give it to a second spectator behind his back. As soon as the handkerchief is out of sight behind his back, tie the one-hand knot described in "The Appearing Knot."

Command the knot to jump from one handkerchief to the other. Snap your fingers. The first spectator brings his handkerchief into view and the knot has vanished. The second spectator brings his handkerchief into view and it is seen that the knot has jumped to the center of his handkerchief.

Either of these knots can also be used in a seance if true darkness can be achieved. The idea here is that if a room is completely dark when the lights are turned out, you can perform a spirit effect. A handkerchief is knotted and dropped into a paper bag. The spectator holds the top of the bag closed. The room lights are turned out for a few seconds, then turned back on. When the spectator removes the handkerchief from the bag, the knot has vanished. Clearly this is the work of spirits who operate in total darkness.

Of course the real secret is that you tied the dissolving knot described in "Not a Knot," and caused the knot to vanish as the handkerchief was being placed in the bag. The rest is a matter of dramatic presentation. In years past the ability of spirits to tie and untie knots in rope and handkerchiefs was considered proof that ghosts existed. It is still an effective presentation.

66. THE KNOT PARADOX

If you grasp the ends of a handkerchief, it is impossible to tie a simple overhand knot in the handkerchief without letting go of the ends. But because it is impossible, magicians have devised a number of ingenious ways to apparently tie a knot without letting go the ends of the handkerchief.

Perhaps the oldest method is the following. Stretch the handkerchief out on a table. Then cross the arms as shown in Figure 104. Grasp one end of the handkerchief in each hand. Pull the

FIG. 104.

left hand to the left and the right hand to the right. The result is that a knot will automatically form in the handkerchief. The trick works because in crossing your arms you have in effect formed a knot with your arms. In uncrossing the arms the knot is transferred to the handkerchief.

67. THE SECOND PARADOX

The above method is something of a gag and it can easily be duplicated by most spectators. When they've done it, ask them if they can figure out another method of tying a knot without letting go of the ends of the handkerchief. When they give up, you demonstrate the following method.

Have a spectator hold a handkerchief by the ends as shown in Figure 105. Cross your arms and grasp the ends as shown in Figure 106. Have the spectator release his grip on the handkerchief.

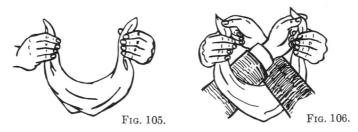

FIG. 105.   FIG. 106.

Uncross your hands and a knot forms in the center of the handkerchief. Done smoothly and fairly quickly, this method will fool even an astute observer.

68. THE THIRD PARADOX

After performing the above two versions, you are ready to perform one of the strongest variations of the "impossible" knot. Place the handkerchief on the table in the form of an inverted U, Figure 107. Grasp end *B* with the right hand.

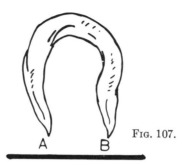

Fig. 107.

Now slip your left hand under the handkerchief, double the hand back as shown by the arrow in Figure 108, and grasp end *A*. Immediately separate your hands and a knot will form in the center of the handkerchief.

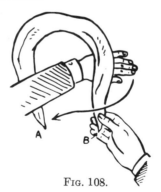

Fig. 108.

At this point ask the spectator to duplicate the knot. If you have performed the three versions described above, the spectator will be completely unable to form the knot. When he gives up, you can repeat the three versions of the knot, but in a different order. If he turns away for a second, you can form the one-hand knot described under "The Appearing Knot," page 78.

Thus when the spectator turns back, there is a knot in the handkerchief. The spectator will be so confused that he will find it impossible to form a knot without letting go of the ends.

69. POPPER UP

In this routine a pencil placed under a handkerchief immediately pops up through the handkerchief. It is a fast, visual penetration.

METHOD: You can use a pencil or a pen, a cigarette or even a breadstick for this trick. In this description we will assume that a pencil is used.

Hold the pencil as shown in Figure 109, between the thumb and third and fourth fingers. The left hand picks up a hand-

Fig. 109.

kerchief at its center and drops it over the pencil. But what actually happens is that the pencil is lowered out of the way and the first and second fingers are covered with the handkerchief.

Now snap the pencil to an upright position. From the front it appears as if the pencil instantly penetrated the handkerchief, Figure 110.

Fig. 110.

Since the pencil protrudes from the back of the handkerchief, when performing the trick make sure the audience is directly in front of you.

70. COMEDY VANISH

If asked to repeat the above trick you can perform this routine as it starts out the same but has a different ending. Based on a classic trick of Martin Gardner's, it appears as if a pencil placed under a handkerchief is made to vanish in an extremely puzzling way. But the trick has a funny and unexpected ending.

Grasp the pencil between the right thumb and second finger. The left hand starts to cover the pencil with a handkerchief. In the process the right first finger is extended and it is actually the first finger that is covered with the handkerchief, Figure 111. As in the previous trick the pencil extends out from the back of the handkerchief.

Fɪɢ. 111.

Raise the handkerchief so it is directly in front of the face. Pretend to grasp the pencil through the handkerchief with the left hand and lift the handkerchief a bit. As you do, move your hands back a bit and grip the pencil between your teeth.

Release your right hand's grip on the pencil and slowly turn your right hand so that the palm is toward the audience, Figure 112. Your left hand then whips the handkerchief off your right hand. From the front it appears as if the pencil has completely vanished, Figure 113. Actually the right hand blocks the audience view of the true situation.

Wait for the applause to stop. Then lower the right hand and

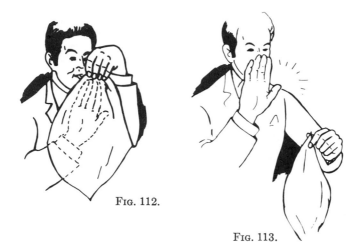

Fig. 112.

Fig. 113.

show that the pencil is in your mouth. It is an amusing and surprising finish to the routine and should earn you another round of applause.

71. FOURTH-DIMENSIONAL HANKS

In this ingenious routine, two handkerchiefs penetrate one another. It is the invention of Edwin Tabor.

If possible use handkerchiefs or scarves of different colors. Place one on the table and a second on top of it at right angles, Figure 114. Grasp end *D* and place it under the shaded handkerchief in the direction of the arrow in Figure 114.

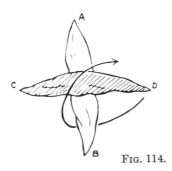

Fig. 114.

You are now at the point of Figure 115. Grasp end *B* and move it in the direction of the arrow in Figure 115. This will bring you to the situation of Figure 116.

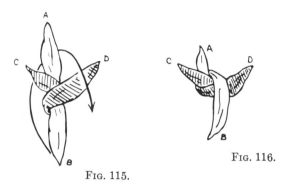

Fig. 115.

Fig. 116.

Place end *C* with end *D* and let the spectator hold these two ends. Place end *A* with end *B* and hold these with your right hand. Place your left first finger at the center of the intertwined handkerchiefs to keep them in place on the table.

Mention that it would be impossible to separate the two handkerchiefs unless you twisted them through the fourth dimension. Slowly and gently pull on the ends of your handkerchief and it will visibly penetrate the other handkerchief.

72. THE MacCARTHY HANK FOLD

In the realm of ingenious magical thinking, E. Brian Mac-Carthy's handkerchief fold rates at the top of the list. It is a utility device which can be applied to a great many different magical effects.

One of the most impressive applications is this. The magician borrows four coins from a spectator. One of the coins is marked. All four coins are dropped into a bag made from a folded handkerchief. The coins are mixed around. Then, without moves, the marked coin penetrates the bag and falls to the table. The other coins remain in the center of the handkerchief.

The above effect was suggested by J. W. Sarles, who pointed out that the apparatus need not be restricted to coins. You can gather keys, rings and other small objects in the handkerchief bag. On command any desired object penetrates the bag and falls to the table or into the spectator's hand.

METHOD: The strength of this method lies in its simplicity. It is set up in front of the spectator, yet it is so well concealed that the real working is never suspected.

Place a handkerchief in front of you as in Figure 117. Bring end A up to meet end B, Figure 118. Then bring corner C over to the right to the position shown in Figure 119. Finally, bring corner D over to the left. The completed fold looks like that shown in Figure 120.

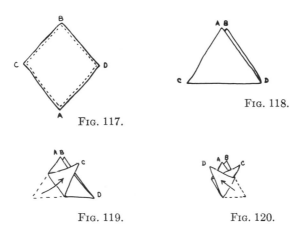

FIG. 117.

FIG. 118.

FIG. 119.

FIG. 120.

From the audience's view you have simply folded a handkerchief to make an impromptu handkerchief bag. But the ingenious construction of the hank fold allows you to steal a coin or other object in the easiest possible manner.

The idea is this. If you hold the handkerchief bag as shown in Figure 121 and drop a coin into compartment x, it will fall into

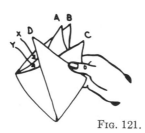

FIG. 121.

the center of the bag. But if you drop a coin into compartment *y* it will *not* fall into the center of the bag. Instead it will drop behind the bag, yet it will still be concealed in the folds of the hank.

After you drop a coin into compartment *y*, reach into the fold at the base of the handkerchief bag with the left thumb, Figure 122, and pull the coin out. It will appear as if the coin has mysteriously penetrated the center of the bag.

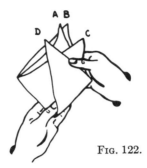

Fig. 122.

This is the basic effect, but it is too obvious if presented this way. To disguise the principle, ask the spectator for several coins. Tell him to mark one of them. As he does this, make the handkerchief bag already described.

Pick up the spectator's coins one at a time and drop them into compartment *x* of the handkerchief bag. Drop the marked coin into compartment *y*. Shake the handkerchief bag gently to mix the coins. Don't shake it too hard or the coin in compartment *y* will fall out.

When ready to complete the effect, contact the bottom of the bag with the right hand, reach into the folds with the thumb and pull the marked coin into view. Then open the bag to show that the other coins remained inside.

The effect can be reversed. Drop the marked coin into compartment *x* and the other three coins into compartment *y*. On command the three unmarked coins penetrate the handkerchief bag, leaving the marked coin inside.

In handling the MacCarthy handkerchief fold you may find that the coin placed in compartment *y* has a tendency to fall out as soon as it's dropped inside. To avoid the problem make sure corners *C* and *D* are held higher than *A* and *B*.

73. TIME FLIES

This spectacular handling of the MacCarthy handkerchief fold was suggested by Slydini, the master close-up magician. It has surprise, drama, comedy and mystery, all of the ingredients of a classic of close-up magic.

Needed is a large man's handkerchief. Fold it into the Mac-Carthy handkerchief bag. As you do, ask for the loan of a few keys, a few coins, and a wristwatch. All of these borrowed objects are dropped into the handkerchief bag.

Then the bag is slammed against the tabletop in a dramatic gesture. Naturally the spectator who loaned you the watch is likely to faint as he mentally pictures his valuable watch being smashed to bits.

He opens the handkerchief bag and is astonished to discover that although the keys and coins are there, his watch has vanished. For the finish, you produce his watch on *your* wrist!

METHOD: Form the handkerchief bag as already described. As you do, ask for the loan of several keys and several coins. The idea here is that you want metal objects which are unbreakable in themselves but which produce a terrific noise when banged against the table.

Drop these objects into compartment x of the handkerchief bag. Ask for the loan of a wristwatch. When you get the watch, pretend to examine it. Say, "This looks like a very expensive watch. I imagine it would cost quite a bit to repair it in the unlikely event that it was damaged." The spectator hears the voice of doom, but it is too late. Drop the watch into compartment y of the handkerchief bag.

Jingle the contents of the bag. Shake your head and say, "It's not enough. We need one more coin. Does someone have a quarter?" This is merely a diversion. As the spectators search their pockets for a coin, lower the handkerchief bag so that the bottom of it is below the level of the tabletop. Your left hand quietly steals the watch from the bag, Figure 123.

Leave the watch in your lap. Take the quarter from the spectator and drop it into compartment x of the handkerchief bag.

Remark that everyone has heard the expression, "Time flies." Say that you will demonstrate what it means. Raise the

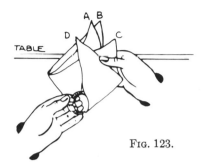

Fig. 123.

handkerchief bag, then smash it down against the tabletop. If it is a wooden table, or if you are afraid of scratching the surface, place a book or newspaper on the table and smash the handkerchief against that.

There will be a predictable reaction from the owner of the watch. He will leap up and open the handkerchief bag to reclaim his no-doubt mangled watch. As all attention is on the handkerchief bag, you have ample opportunity to slip the watch onto your wrist. Keep your hands below the level of the tabletop as you do this. Also, keep your elbows against your sides so there will be little visible movement as you slip the watch on your wrist.

At this point the spectators will realize that the watch has vanished from inside the handkerchief. Stand up, push the coins and keys aside as if helping the spectator search for his watch, look behind you, pat your pockets, then say, "I'm really sorry about your watch. I haven't a clue as to what happened to it. Why don't you take mine."

The watch that is apparently yours is removed from your wrist and handed to the spectator. He will be astonished to discover that you have handed him back his own watch.

On occasion the spectator will tell you that he doesn't want your watch, he wants his own. Even when you jokingly say, "But mine is just like yours," he may not believe you are actually handing him back his own watch. This sets up an amusing situation that only adds to the entertainment value of the routine.

CLOSE-UP ILLUSIONS

Whereas the stage magician must rely on special apparatus to perform his illusions, the close-up magician is always ready to perform because he uses borrowed props in an impromptu setting.

In this chapter we will describe, among other secrets, how to stretch your finger, how to float a toothpick, and what happens when an ordinary card is twisted through the fifth dimension.

74. DEXTEROUS DIGITS

The magician succeeds in stretching his little finger until it is as long as his first finger. Then he shrinks it back to normal size again.

METHOD: Hold your right hand palm-up and call attention to the fact that the little finger is aptly named since it is the smallest finger. "As you can see, it's about an inch smaller than my first finger." As you say this, point to the disparity in size, Figure 124.

"But if I stretch it like this, an odd thing happens." Turn the right hand palm down and tug on the right little finger with the left thumb and first finger. Then display the palm-down right hand as shown in Figure 125.

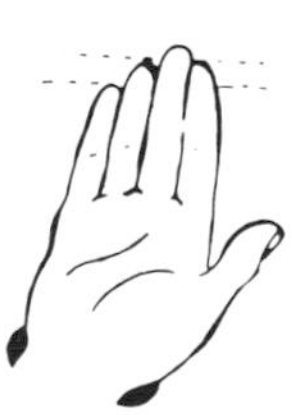

FIG. 124. 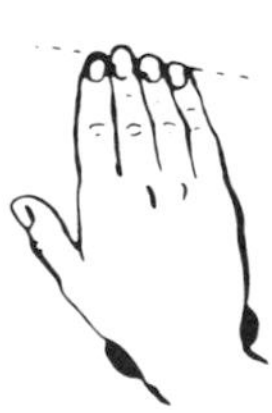   FIG. 125.

If you try this and hold your hand as shown in Figure 125, the little finger will actually be almost the same size as the first finger. The reason is based on a well concealed secret, and it is that the right hand has been twisted or angled to the right. Keep the right arm stationary and twist the hand at the wrist. Properly performed, it appears as if the little finger has suddenly become the same length as the first finger.

Turn the right hand palm-up again. "I'd better push it back to its normal size." As this is said, grasp the right little finger with the left thumb and first finger. Pretend to push the right little finger. Then display you right hand as in Figure 124 again. The little finger is now back to its normal size.

The above presentation is a variation of an idea of George Starke's.

75. IT FLOATS!

The performer borrows an ordinary toothpick and then causes it to float mysteriously in the air. A match can be used in place of a toothpick. This routine is a logical sequel to "The Penetrating Matches," page 23.

METHOD: This is actually a combination of two secrets. Borrow a toothpick and hold it in your clenched left fist. Grasp your left wrist with your right hand. The situation is shown in Figure 126. Note however that the right first finger does not show in Figure 126. It is behind your left hand.

When you open your left hand, the toothpick appears to be suspended in the air, Figure 127. The true situation is shown from in back, Figure 128. The right first finger actually holds the toothpick in place.

FIG. 126.

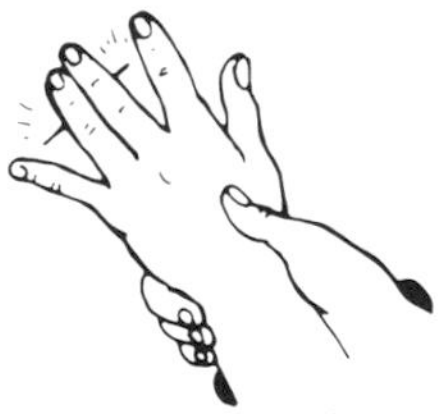

FIG. 127.

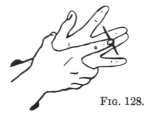

Fig. 128.

If the left second and third fingers are kept together, they screen the presence of the right first finger. The illusion from in front is perfect. Just be sure no one stands at your right because they will see how it's done.

This is a more or less standard trick and can be done with a pencil, a pen or any similar object. But the follow-up trick, in which the object appears to float and dance in the air, can be done only with a slender, lightweight object like a toothpick. Here are the details.

Hold the toothpick between the thumbs as in Figure 129. Curl the fingers in and interlock them, but do so with the right middle finger in back of the other fingers as shown in Figure 130.

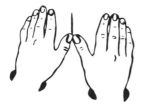

Fig. 129.

Fig. 130.

Wedge the toothpick under the fingernail of the right middle finger. Then move the thumbs apart. The result is shown in Figure 131, a perfect illusion of a floating toothpick.

Fig. 131.

Slowly move the right finger back and forth. The toothpick will appear to dance in the air. Let the toothpick float for a few seconds, then reverse the above handling to bring it back to the situation of Figure 129.

76. AN OPTICAL TRICK

There are many optical illusions which trick the eye and fool the mind. This is an outstanding example. Two pieces of paper or cardboard of the same length are placed at right angles to one another as shown in Figure 132. Then the magician picks up one piece and stretches it so it is longer than the other. The piece actually *is* longer as can be verified by the spectator.

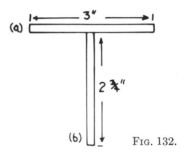

Fig. 132.

METHOD: Actually the secret to this trick has already been explained. If you study Figure 132 closely you will see that the pieces of paper are not the same length. Piece *a* is about three inches long, while piece *b* is two and three-quarters inches in length. But by placing the pieces at right angles as in Figure 132, the pieces of paper appear to be the same length. This is the key to the mystery.

To perform the trick, place the pieces at right angles as in Figure 132. Then pick up piece *a* and pretend to stretch it by tugging gently on it. Then place it against piece *b*, but in the manner indicated in Figure 133. Now it looks as if piece *a* is much longer than piece *b*.

Finally pick up *a*, saying, "I did't mean to stretch it that much." Blow on it, then place it alongside *b* (that is, parallel to *b*), to show that it is still longer than *b*, though not quite as much as before.

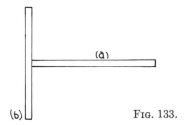

FIG. 133.

The trick can be done with two pencils or any similar objects which can be cut to the correct proportions. From time to time the trick has been done with cigarettes. The long cigarette is king-sized and the short cigarette is regular-sized. In any case, the handling is the same as given above.

77. WHISK AWAY

Some illusions are based on sound. The sense of hearing, rather than the sense of sight, is tricked by the magician. In the following curious illusion you use two spectators and a whisk broom. This unlikely combination produces a trick that will puzzle the audience and astound one of the assisting spectators.

The two spectators stand facing the audience. You stand in back of the assisting spectators. In your hand is a whisk broom. You explain that you would like to try a little game to test the reflexes of the assistants. You are going to brush the whisk broom against one spectator's back. Before you have brushed his back three times he is to reach behind him and grasp the whisk broom.

It's a simple test that appears vaguely logical. You begin to brush the whisk broom against one spectator's back. He grabs for the broom, but grasps only your right hand. The brush is in the *other* hand.

METHOD: The method is simply explained, but you will have to try it (or have it tried on you) to convince yourself just how remarkable the illusion is. The secret is this. With the two spectators standing in front of you facing the audience, grasp the whisk broom in your left hand and brush the back of the spectator on your left.

But at the same time brush your right hand against the back

of the spectator on your right. Synchronize the motion of both hands and the spectator on the right will swear that it is his back which is being brushed with the whisk broom. The spectator hears the sound of the broom and he feels something brushing against his back. His mind places the two sensory inputs together and he concludes that it is his back which is being brushed with the whisk broom.

The audience cannot see clearly what you are doing because you are standing behind the two spectators. But they will see that the spectator on the right grabbed your hand and they will be puzzled that he thought his back was being brushed with the whisk broom. The spectator on the right will be amazed to grab for the whisk broom and find only your empty hand. It is a strange aural illusion.

78. LOOKING-GLASS LOGIC

The saying that it's all done with mirrors is literally correct in this trick since a mirror is the major item of apparatus. The patter line, suggested by R. M. Jamison, is, "I have a rare mirror, a piece of *Alice Through the Looking Glass* mirror. Things are a bit different in Looking Glass Land. Let me show you an example."

The apparatus consists of a hand mirror or pocket mirror and several slips of paper or pieces of cardboard on which you have printed words and numbers. When the spectator looks at the printed words, he sees one sentence, but when he looks at the mirror image he sees a different sentence. The transformations are surprising and amusing. Once the idea is grasped, the reader can invent many variations.

METHOD: The following material is taken largely from ideas suggested by Martin Gardner. To grasp the basic idea, first note that certain letters of the alphabet do not appear reversed when viewed in a mirror. The following capital letters are non-reversible: B, C, D, E, H, I, K, O, X. If a word is made from some of these letters, it will not be reversed in a mirror.

To take a simple example, print the word BOB on a piece of paper. Hold a pocket mirror upright in the hand, keeping it in place with the thumb. Place the paper on the fingertips and look at the mirror image of the writing, Figure 134. You will find that the mirror image of BOB is BOB.

Fɪɢ. 134.

The classic example of mirror writing is printed on a package of Camel cigarettes. Look at the words Choice Quality on the pack, then look at the same words in a mirror. Quality is reversed but Choice is not. For those unfamiliar with the basic idea, it is startling to see one word reversed and the other perfectly readable in the mirror.

Using the above letters one can form words and sentences which do not reverse in a mirror. For example, DID BOB KICK ED reads correctly when viewed in a mirror. But to add an element of mystery, some sort of transformation should take place. The following idea has been suggested. Write the words CHOICE QUALITY on a piece of paper, but write CHOICE with red ink and QUALITY with blue or black ink. Explain that you have a new type infrared mirror which is sensitive only to certain wavelengths of light. Hold the paper up to the mirror. The black writing is reversed as it should be, but the red writing is not. I believe the use of different color inks was suggested by Louis Histed.

To elaborate on the Looking Glass theme, there are a number of amusing sentences that can be made up. First, print ED DID HIDE, WOW on a piece of paper. Show it to the spectator, saying that it was the headline in a famous missing-persons case. To solve the case, detectives had only to peer into the Looking Glass. Hold the paper in your right hand, thumb on top, fingers below. Cover the comma after the word HIDE with the right thumb as you place the paper near the mirror, Figure 135. When the spectator looks into the mirror he sees the solution to the case: ED DID HIDE MOM.

Remark that the Looking Glass also explains why one store-keeper was fined for overcharging. Show a piece of paper which has the words CHOICE DICE—50¢ written on it as shown in

Fɪɢ. 135.

Figure 136. When the spectator looks at the mirror image of the writing he finds the real price because now the words read CHOICE DICE—20¢.

The next example uses some lower case letters as well as capital letters. As shown in Figure 137, you display the words Bob Kicked Pop. To find out *why* he did it, look at the mirror image of the writing.

CHOICE   DICE - 50¢   bob KICKED POP

Fɪɢ. 136.   Fɪɢ. 137.

Finally, there is the surprising fact that some numbers become letters when viewed in a mirror. The best example is this one suggested by Martin Gardner. The addition problem of Figure 138 is obviously wrong, but you explain that it's really a

$$7192$$
$$H1$$
$$3HT$$
$$\overline{HOOTT192}$$

Fɪɢ. 138.

code. To break the code, view the numbers upside down in a mirror. The result is surprising and amusing, and forms a good finish for a mirror-writing routine.

The reader may wish to experiment with other ideas. For example, one can secretly add lines to the mirror. These lines will merge with the mirror-image letters to form completely different words. The other avenue of exploration is relatively new to this subject. It rests on the fact that certain pictures, when viewed upside down, transform into completely different pictures. This is especially easy to do with cartoon renditions of faces. The subject is too lengthy to go into here, but the reader will surely profit from experimentation.

79. HYPERCARD

One of the newest paradoxes is a strange and seemingly impossible configuration known as Hypercard. Using an ordinary file card, giving it a couple of cuts and folds, you end up with the card as shown in Figure 139. Before going further, you may want to try to figure out how it is possible to arrive at such a configuration using a single file card that remains in one piece throughout.

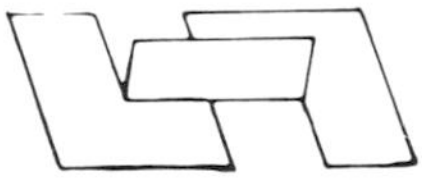

FIG. 139.

The problem appears impossible because the center panel is at right angles to the rest of the card. But if the problem is simplified, the solution becomes obvious. If, for instance, you were asked to cut a file card to form the configurate of Figure 140, you would have no problem. This is actually the solution to Hypercard also, except that the cuts made in the card are different.

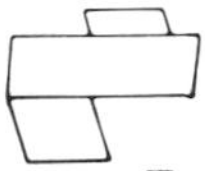

FIG. 140.

To form Hypercard, divide the file card into eighths by folding it along the dotted lines shown in Figure 141, then make the cuts from A, B and C to the center line. Give the right half of the card a half-turn, Figure 142, and you will have constructed Hypercard.

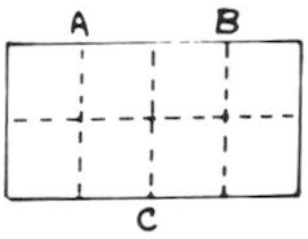

FIG. 141.

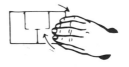

FIG. 142.

It can be used just this way. Have someone initial the left side of an uncut card. Fold the card into eighths, then place the card below the level of the tabletop, make the required cuts with a pair of scissors, give the right half a twist, then bring Hypercard into view. Show it on all sides, then place it in your pocket. Hand the spectator another file card and a pair of scissors. Challenge him to form a Hypercard. He will almost certainly find it impossible.

80. THE FIFTH DIMENSION

In the form given above, Hypercard is a puzzle. But you can make a magic trick out of it by using a clever idea suggested by Mel Stover and Howard Lyons. This is to perform part of the cutting operation prior to the performance of the trick, and then concealing this fact. The following is a handling based on the Stover-Lyons premise. In this trick a set of initials written on the card by a spectator seem to change their position.

To prepare the file card, divide it into eights as before, then place your initials on the back of the card in the position shown in Figure 143. To complete the prior preparation, use the scissors to make a cut from C to the center of the card. The result looks like Figure 144.

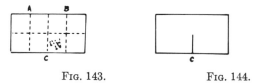

FIG. 143.   FIG. 144.

In presenting the routine, hold the file card with your right thumb covering the cut at the center. Then openly cut from A to the center and from B to the center. The result will look like Figure 145. Remember that this cutting is done openly but the audience is unaware of the cut concealed by the thumb. Also, they do not know that your initials are on the bottom of the card.

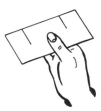

FIG. 145.

Now fold the center panel down toward you as shown in Figure 146. Slip the right thumb on top of the panel to keep it in place. The panel now conceals the secret cut in the file card.

FIG. 146.

Have the spectator initial the upper-left corner of the card. Hold the center panel down with your left hand. Then openly initial the right corner. Make these initials look like the secret initials on the back of the card. The situation thus far looks like Figure 147.

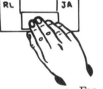

FIG. 147.

Using both hands, and taking care to keep the center panel in place, pick up the file card. Then grasp it as shown in Figure 148, thumb on top, fingers below. Remark that in order to get

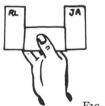

FIG. 148.

the initials closer together, you must pass the card though the fifth dimension. Still holding the card as in Figure 148, place it below the level of the tabletop and out of the spectator's line of vision.

Grip the card with both hands as shown in Figure 149. While your left hand remains stationary your right hand turn palm down with its section of the card. The result of this action is shown in Figure 150. The initials that were secretly written on the underside of the card are now in view.

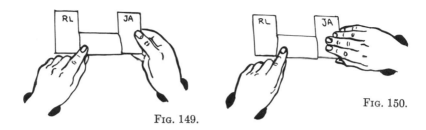

Fig. 149.

Fig. 150.

The left hand now releases the center panel. The result is the seemingly impossible Hypercard of Figure 151. Bring the card up into view and rest it on the table so that the spectator can

Fig. 151.

clearly see the result. His initials are indeed closer to yours than they were at the start, and the center of the card is now standing upright and at right angles to the rest of the card. Point to the center panel and say, "This is the trapdoor, and you know that all magic is done with trapdoors."

Note that by having the spectator initial the card, you have dispelled the possible suspicion that you switched out the original card and switched in a special card. This only adds to the astonishing result.

THE LINKING PINS

One of the most recent additions to the literature of magic is the subject of tricks where safety pins magically link and unlink. Perhaps the newness of the subject is due to the fact that safety pins in their present form are themselves an invention of fairly recent times, yet already there is a substantial body of material on the subject of safety-pin magic.

The basic effect is that two safety pins, honestly linked together, are made to instantaneously unlink. What is remarkable about the trick is that there are no gimmicks or sleights. Several variations on the theme will be given in this chapter, including an uncanny version where the pins unlink while held in a spectator's hand. The chapter closes with a Pin Through Handkerchief that is a brilliant example of original thinking in this field.

81. SAFETY PIN-UP

The effect is as already described: two safety pins, honestly linked together, instantly unlink. It is best to begin with a brief statement of the nomenclature, most of which was suggested by J. G. Thompson, Jr. This nomenclature will be used throughout the chapter to describe the handling.

Try to obtain pins as large as possible. Blanket pins are excellent because they are easily obtainable, and being of a large size, add to the visibility of the trick. The head and spring ends of the pin are indicated in Figure 152. The pin is the pointed end that moves in and out of the head. The bar is the stationary segment permanently fastened to the head.

Newer pins usually work best in tricks of this type. Older pins tend to lose their springiness and will sometimes open

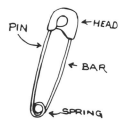

FIG. 152.

inadvertently during the handling of the trick. In all of these tricks it is important that the pins be linked and held exactly as shown in the illustrations. The handling is easy and certain, but only if the instructions are followed exactly.

To perform the basic unlinking trick, hold a closed pin in the right hand. Link the other pin through it as shown in Figure 153. Make sure the audience is aware that the pins are securely linked. Then grasp them as shown in Figure 154. Pull them apart with a quick sharp motion and the pins will unlink instantly. If you try this with the apparatus in hand you will probably fool yourself the first time you try it.

FIG. 153.

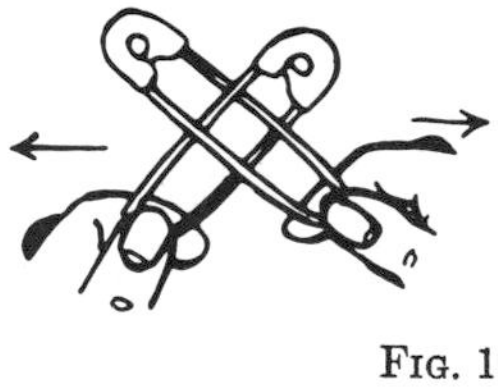

FIG. 154.

82. SWINDLE PINS

When you perform "Safety Pin-Up," the audience is likely to ask you to repeat the trick. Repeat it once more as described above. You can if you like use a variation in linking the pins. This is shown in Figure 155. With the pins linked this way, pull them sharply and they will unlink.

Now offer to demonstrate the trick one more time. But here you switch to a swindle suggested by Don White. Pretend to link the pins once more, but actually engage them as shown in Figure 156. With the pins closed and held as in Figure 157, it

Fig. 155.

Fig. 156.

Fig. 157.

appears as if the pins are linked, but really they are not. Turn both pins over and hold them as shown in Figure 158. Remark that whereas before you unlinked them at the head end, this time you will try to unlink them at the spring end.

Pull the pins apart and of course they magically separate. Anyone who tries to duplicate the effect is doomed to failure.

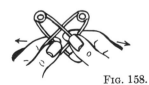

Fig. 158.

83. THE IMPOSSIBLE UNLINK

If the audience asks to see more safety pin magic, you can present them with a truly impossible-seeming effect invented by Tom Ellis. It requires a few minutes practice to get the handling, but the effect is worth the small investment in time. Start with the left-hand pin open. Insert the point of the pin through the spring of the right-hand pin, Figure 159. Close the left-hand pin. The pins are now obviously linked in such a way that to unlink them seems impossible.

FIG. 159.

To unlink them, your right hand moves its pin to the right until the spring is adjacent to the head of the left-hand pin, Figure 160. Your left hand holds its pin firmly in place as your

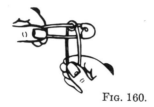

FIG. 160.

right hand turns its pin in toward the body and continues to rotate the pin up and away from the body over the top of the left-hand pin.

The right-hand pin is rotated a half-revolution around the left-hand pin. If done slowly, you will see the spring of the right-hand safety pin pull the pin of the left-hand safety pin out of the head, Figure 161.

FIG. 161.

The right-hand pin is now pulled to the right and free of the left-hand pin. When performing, use a little up and down motion of the hands to cover the unlink. This motion conceals the actual working and makes the trick look impossible.

84. THE REPEAT IMPOSSIBILITY

If asked to repeat a trick it is always wise to have a different method in readiness. Thus, no matter how closely the audience watches, even though they think they are seeing a repeat demonstration, they cannot follow the trick because you are in fact doing a different trick.

Tom Ellis devised this method of following "The Impossible Unlink." Insert the pin point of the open left-hand pin through the spring of the right-hand pin and then close the left-hand pin. The situation is shown in Figure 162.

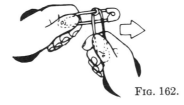

FIG. 162.

Bear down just a bit with the left thumb. This has the effect of pushing the pin of the left-hand safety pin down slightly and makes the unlink easier. When you gain familiarity with the trick you will find this step unnecessary. After the pin has been pushed down slightly, pull the right-hand safety pin sharply to the right in the direction of the arrow in Figure 162 and it will unlink from the other safety pin.

This method requires a bit of practice to get the knack. Pressure must be firm and the right hand must move quickly to the right for the unlink to work.

85. UN-SAFETY PINS

This is one of the strangest tricks which can be done with unprepared safety pins. Two closed safety pins are placed in a spectator's fist. Explaining that these are un-safety pins, the performer says that the name derives from the fact that the pins insist on opening themselves.

The spectator is asked to slowly and gently open his fist a bit. As he does he will experience an uncanny sensation because he will feel the safety pins twist and turn in his hand as they magically open themselves!

METHOD: This trick was invented by Jerry Andrus. It is not quite impromptu because of the way the pins are set up at the start. But a good plan is to do several of the tricks in this chapter, then act as if the performance is finished. As you talk about some other subject, pretend to absently handle the pins. Actually you arrange it so that the pointed end of each pin is secured under the head of the other pin, Figure 163.

Fig. 163.

Holding the pins as in the illustration, place them in a spectator's hand. Don't let go of them until he closes his hand into a tight fist. Then explain that these are un-safety pins because they insist on opening up by themselves.

Have the spectator loosen his fist a bit. As he does, the pins will twist and turn in his hand until they open themselves. Have him open his hand and the two open pins will fall out onto the table.

Before doing the trick it is a good idea to file down the pointed ends so they have been dulled. This will prevent the spectator from getting scratched by one of the pin points.

86. QUICK RELEASE

Fasten one safety pin to the right edge of a spectator's jacket (with his consent, of course). Then slide another safety pin through a buttonhole on the left side of his jacket and link the two pins together.

Tell the spectator to close his eyes, grasp the pins and unlink them. He is to do it as fast as possible. Have someone time the spectator. To insure that he must fumble a bit opening the pins, have him close his eyes before you explain the object of the trick. This way he won't know quite how the pins are linked and it will take him that extra few seconds to get them untangled.

Regardless of how quickly he unfastens the pins, tell him you will better his time. Fasten the pins together again, but in the manner described in "Safety Pin-Up." Ask the spectator who is keeping time if he is ready. He says yes. Then you instantly unlink the pins, using the method described in "Safety Pin-Ups." Until this point it appears to be a simple game, but with the instant release it becomes a puzzling bit of magic.

87. PIN-A-TRATION

Two linked safety pins are placed inside a handkerchief. One at a time the pins penetrate the handkerchief. All articles may be borrowed.

METHOD: Actually the routine combines two ideas already described in this book. Make an impromptu handkerchief bag using the MacCarthy Hank Fold described on page 86.

After doing one or two unlinking tricks with the safety pins, pretend to link them together, but actually use the fake method described in "Swindle Pins," page 104.

Hold the pins in one hand and pick up the handkerchief bag with the other. Drop the two apparently-linked pins into the handkerchief bag, allowing the pins to go into compartment y. Shake the bag to allow the pins to fall to the bottom. Then reach up with your free hand to the bottom of the bag, insert your thumb into the fold and remove one of the pins with a snap. Then remove the other pin.

The audience is thus faced with a double mystery. Not only have the safety pins penetrated the handkerchief bag, they have unlinked from one another in the process.

88. ULTRA PENETRO

After performing "Pin-A-Tration" you are ready to perform a knock-out penetration that seemingly has no answer. What the audience sees is a series of logical actions leading inexorably to a remarkable conclusion.

This trick is the invention of Richard Durham. As seen by the audience, the magician borrows a handkerchief, folds it in half and pins a safety pin through the center of the handkerchief. He then opens the handkerchief to show that the pin is fairly pinned to the fabric.

Again folding the handkerchief, the magician proceeds to wrap the handkerchief around the pin, but leaving one end of the pin in full view. After the handkerchief is completely wrapped around the pin, the magician has the spectator pull the safety pin. Now, believe it or not, the safety pin slides completely free of the handkerchief.

What is most unexpected about this trick in terms of method is that there are no hidden moves and no handling other than what the audience sees. Thus we have a trick that looks impossible yet is completely self-working.

METHOD: Any borrowed handkerchief may be used, but when you first practice the trick, make sure you use an inexpensive cotton handkerchief. The reason is that if you make a mistake or are not too sure of the handling, the handkerchief may snag or tear. When you become familiar with the handling you can do the trick with any handkerchief.

The handkerchief is folded in half and the pin passed through the double handkerchief at about the center and down about a half-inch from the fold, Figure 164. Open out the handkerchief

FIG. 164.

so the head of the pin is away from you, then turn the handkerchief over and spread it out on the table with the pin underneath. All that shows is a portion of the pin as indicated in Figure 165. Be sure that the head of the safety pin is toward you.

FIG. 165.

Grasp the top of the handkerchief and fold it toward you so the spring end of the pin shows. Taking hold of the safety pin at the Spring end, turn it over and over, thereby wrapping the handkerchief around the pin, Figure 166.

Take hold of the spring end of the safety pin and pull. Impossible as it may seem, the pin will slide free of the handkerchief.

PIN
WRAPPED
IN HANKY

Fig. 166.

PEN-ULTIMATE MAGIC

Perhaps because the magic wand has so long been associated with magic, tricks using objects of similar shape have occupied a prominent place in the literature. Routines using wands, knives, pens, pencils, even cigars and canes, form an important part of the art of close-up magic.

In this final chapter we will consider some of the classic stunts and puzzles on the subject, and close with a number of magical routines. In some of the tricks a pencil will be used and in others a pen, but in most cases objects of similar shape and size can be substituted. In keeping with the approach used throughout this book, there are no special gimmicks or sleights. So, if you have nothing to work with but a pencil and you know the tricks in this chapter alone, you are ready to perform a complete close-up act of fine magic.

89. BUTTONHOLED

This classic stunt is believed to have been invented by Sam Loyd. The present version uses a ballpoint pen with a cap and a length of string. Once this impromptu version is made up and the principle understood, you can make up a more permanent version, as will be explained later.

Assuming the pen is about 5½ inches in length, take a piece of string about 9 inches long, tie the ends so a loop is formed, and jam the loop between the pen and the cap, Figure 167. The pen-and-loop combination can now be threaded through a

Fig. 167.

spectator's buttonhole in such a way that the spectator will find it impossible to remove the apparatus.

Start with the apparatus as shown in Figure 168. The loop is behind the spectator's buttonhole. Pull the cloth through the

FIG. 168.

loop until you are able to push the pen through the buttonhole, Figure 169. The result is that the apparatus is "locked" onto the spectator's buttonhole, Figure 170, and can't be removed unless the spectator knows the secret.

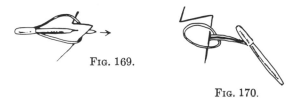

FIG. 169.

FIG. 170.

METHOD: The secret is to reverse the actions described above. But in practice, don't do this. Instead, when the spectator gives up, remove the cap from pen, pull the loop free of his buttonhole, then reset the apparatus as in Figure 167.

Now if the spectator asks you to repeat the stunt, or if someone else asks you to do it for him, they might glimpse how you got the apparatus hooked onto the buttonhole, but they won't know how to get it off.

As to why it works, what is involved here is a triangle, with the pen forming one side, the string another, and the jacket another. As you draw the jacket through the loop you are making one side of the triangle longer and longer. When it is long enough, the pencil can be worked through the string to dissolve the loop.

A more permanent version of "Buttonholed" can be made from a ruler with a hole drilled through it at one end. The loop of string has to be shorter than the ruler. The handling is the same as given above.

90. LOOPHOLE LOGIC

In the unlikely event that a spectator knows how "Button-holed" works, there is a subtle way to mislead him, using his knowledge to work against him. The apparatus is the same, but instead of looping the apparatus through a buttonhole, you will loop it through the handle of a teacup.

The loop of string must be at least as long as the circum-ference of the cup. If it is, you can loop the apparatus through the handle so it looks like Figure 171. The clever angle here is that if the spectator tries to slide the pen through the loop of string, the method that worked in "Buttonholed," he will find it impossible to apply that thinking here.

Fig. 171.

The way it's done was suggested by Ken Allen. Push a loop of string through the handle of the cup, Figure 172, then draw it completely over the cup, Figure 173, and you will have the ap-paratus locked onto the cup as in Figure 171. Keep this method in reserve for the fellow who knows "Buttonholed," and you will be able to spring on him a baffling close-up mystery.

Fig. 172.   Fig. 173.

91. THE SNAPPER

The invention of G. W. Hunter, this is more of an amusing gag than a trick. Remarking that he is always losing the cap to his pen, the magician says, "But recently I found a pen where the cap can't come off. Darndest thing. I can't figure out how it works."

The magician removes the pen from his pocket. He pulls the cap partway off, lets go, and immediately the cap snaps back onto the pen. He does it a few more times and each time the cap snaps back. When the spectator tries it, the cap does nothing.

METHOD: Hold the pen as shown in Figure 174. Pull the cap about halfway off the pen. To make it snap back, apply pressure with the thumb and finger. The cap will "squirt" back onto the pen. It looks as if there is an elastic connecting the cap to the pen. The audience will assume this, but when they try it the cap doesn't move.

Fig. 174.

92. THE HANDS ONLY

In this stunt you use a pen or pencil plus your hands. The pencil is held as in Figure 175. You give the hands a smooth twist and the pencil ends up as shown in Figure 176. The stunt looks simple, yet when spectators try it, they find it impossible to duplicate.

Fig. 175.

Fig. 176.

When you get the pencil back you repeat the stunt, but this time the pencil breaks in half and then vanishes!

METHOD: Hold the pencil as in Figure 175. There is one crucial move that makes the transition to Figure 176 smooth and easy. This is to cross one thumb over the other as shown in Figure

177. Continue moving the right hand to the position of Figure 178 and then to the end position of Figure 176. A reversal of these moves will bring the pencil back to the starting situation shown in Figure 175.

FIG. 177.   FIG. 178.

After the spectator has tried the trick a few times, take back the pencil and position it as in Figure 175. Repeat the moves and bring the pencil to the position of Figure 176. Then rest your hands at the table's edge and allow secretly the pencil to drop into your lap, Figure 179.

FIG. 179.

Say, "Here's another puzzle. The idea is to divide the pencil into two exactly equal pieces." Raise your hands above the table and make a breaking motion, Figure 180. Then open your hands to show that the pencil has vanished. Thus a clever close-up stunt has been converted to a surprising magical effect.

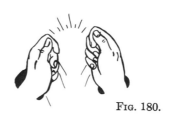

FIG. 180.

93. INVISIBLE INK

"A secret agent gave me this pen as a gift. He said it writes with invisible ink." As you say this display a pen and cover it with a handkerchief.

"But I think there's been a mix-up. It's not the ink that's invisible but the pen." Here you shake out the handkerchief and the pen has vanished!

METHOD: Hold the apparatus as shown in Figure 181. As you place the pen under the handkerchief, allow it to pivot to a horizontal position and slip it into the left sleeve of your jacket.

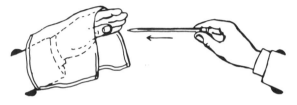

Fig. 181.

Your right hand continues moving up under the handkerchief as if it held the pen. The right forefinger is extended and your left hand allows the handkerchief to drape over the right hand. Your left hand grasps the apparent pen through the cloth, Figure 182.

PENCIL IN SLEEVE

Fig. 182.

Your right hand then moves out from under the handkerchief, grasps a corner and flicks the handkerchief at just the point where you say, "It's not the ink that's invisible but the pen." The pen has vanished.

To produce the pen (a good idea if it's a borrowed pen and you want to retain the friendship of the fellow who loaned it to you) drop your left hand into your left trouser pocket. The pen will slide down the sleeve and into the hand. Pretend to produce the pen from your trouser pocket.

94. PEN KINK

A fine trick invented by Martin Gardner, "Pen Kink" forms the basis for the last routine in this book. As the audience sees it, you explain that you like to give people your autograph because you gain by the experience. As you patter, borrow a spectator's pen, write something on a piece of paper, then return the pen to *your* jacket pocket.

The spectator will naturally object, but then you produce the pen from *his* jacket pocket. It is a quick, bewildering trick.

METHOD: The only requirement is that you be wearing a jacket. Take the pen from the spectator and on a slip of paper write, "Thanks for the pen." Now your right hand seems to place the pen in your inside left jacket pocket. But really you allow the pen to slide down the left jacket sleeve. This idea, done with a coin, was originated by Arthur Finley.

The spectator will of course object, but before he has a chance to say much, you say, "All I need is for you to cosign this paper." Show him the slip of paper with your right hand.

As you do this, allow the left hand to drop to the side. The pen will slide down into your waiting left hand. Since the spectator is sure to raise loud objections by this time, reach into his jacket pocket with the pen and produce it from his pocket.

95. WRITE OFF

If you have just performed "Pen Kink" and want to repeat the trick, this gag, devised by the author, allows for a different ending. You have just returned the pen to the spectator and have performed some other trick. Then you ask for the loan of the pen again to perform a trick such as "Popper Up" (page 83).

At the conclusion of that trick, return the pen to your pocket, then remember that it belongs to the spectator. Hand it back to him and apologize by saying, "I keep thinking this pen ought to belong to me."

The spectator takes the pen, then realizes that is has changed to a pencil!

METHOD: In your inside jacket pocket is a pencil about six inches in length. It rests point-up in the pocket. This is the only preparation.

Borrow the spectator's pen. It must be a ballpoint pen with a cap. Perform "Popper Up." Then place the cap back on the pen. Holding the pen with the cap end up, place the pen in your inside pocket. Say, "Wait a minute. I made this mistake before." As you speak, remove the cap from the pen and place it on the end of the pencil. This is done with the apparatus inside the jacket, so the spectator is unaware that you are transferring the cap to the pencil.

Remove the pencil so that only the cap shows, Figure 183. Say, "I keep thinking it ought to be my pen," and hand it over. Go on to some other trick. The spectator opens his hand and discovers that you've given him back *his* cap on *your* pencil.

FIG. 183.

96. INK OF ANOTHER COLOR

There is an old gag where the magician, removing a pen from his pocket, says that this remarkable pen can write any color called for. Someone calls out "Red," and the magician simply writes the word "Red" on a piece of paper. The following trick is a literal application of this gag, except that in this case you cause the spectator's pen to actually write in a different color ink.

METHOD: In your inside jacket pocket you have a pen that writes with, say, red ink or green ink. The color should be any color except black or blue, and the pen should be of the inexpensive variety found in common use. This means that the pen is likely to match the spectator's pen, and that is the situation you wait for.

Do some trick like "Popper Up" with the spectator's pen, put the pen in your inside jacket pocket and switch the cap to the other pen. Remove this pen from your pocket, apologize for taking his pen, and hand it to the spectator. Immediately do some other trick, say a coin trick.

If his pen matches yours in appearance he probably won't notice the switch. This means that you can now perform a strange trick where the ink apparently changes color. Hand the spectator a piece of paper. Tell him to take his pen out of his pocket, put the paper behind his back and write the word "Red" on the paper.

Then he gives the pen to you. Take another piece of paper, turn your back and write "Red" on the paper. With your back still turned, secretly drop this pen into your inside pocket and bring out the spectator's pen. Hand his pen back to him and tell him to put it in his pocket as it won't be needed.

Have him read what's written on your paper. He reads the word "Red" and also notes that the word was written with red ink. Remark that this is unusual in that his pen writes only in blue ink. He may think it's a gag of some kind, but when he checks the piece of paper he wrote on and still has in his possession, he finds that the word "Red" was written with red ink. Thus he is faced with the impossibility of his own pen writing in a different color ink.

97. PEN ULTIMATE

The most successful magic is that which is amusing and visual, and which can be performed standing with people all around you. This brilliant routine, invented by Howard Wurst, is just such a trick. The plot is simple, the effects are surprising, and the finish is both funny and baffling.

The routine is this. You display a pencil and openly drop it down the right jacket sleeve. Naturally the pencil slides down the sleeve and falls into the right hand.

Again you drop the pencil down the right jacket sleeve. But this time it emerges from the *left* sleeve. It is the same pencil and can be marked prior to performance.

The pencil is now dropped down the jacket's left sleeve. It emerges from the bottom of this sleeve. This is not surprising, but suddenly the magician stretches the pencil so that it is now three times its original size!

METHOD: The trick is not quite impromptu since it is necessary to carry two pencils of similar appearance in the pocket. The first is a pencil that can be comfortably palmed in the hand. This pencil should be about four or five inches in length, although the length will be determined by the size of the hand.

The other pencil should have an eraser end that matches the eraser end of the small pencil. If both pencils are new, the eraser ends will match. This pencil is nine or ten inches long. The actual length is determined by one factor; you are going to drop this pencil down the left sleeve of your jacket and it must sit comfortably inside the sleeve between the shoulder and elbow.

Carry both pencils in the inside left pocket of your jacket. Just prior to performance, secretly remove the large pencil from the pocket and drop it down the sleeve. Keep your elbow bent and the large pencil will rest inside the sleeve between the shoulder and elbow. This prior preparation can be accomplished while you turn your back during a previous trick or when you have the opportunity to leave the room for a moment.

With the preparation complete, remove the small pencil from the pocket. Display it with the left hand. Remember to keep your left hand bent at the elbow. After showing the small pencil, openly drop it down the jacket's right sleeve.

Your right arm is lowered so the pencil is allowed to slide down and into your right hand, Figure 184. Display the pencil. Then transfer it to the left hand again.

Fig. 184.

You are apparently going to repeat the same action. Say, "Magicians are accused of using their sleeves, and that's because they do. This is how they practice." Turn your right side to the audience. Pretend to drop the pencil down the right sleeve, but retain it in your left hand. Your left hand comes out loosely cupped and drops to the left side. But all attention is on the right hand as you shake the arm and apparently allow the pencil to drop down the sleeve.

The audience anticipates the pencil will appear in the right hand. Act puzzled, then say, "It fell down my *left* sleeve." Look at the left hand, open your left hand and show the pencil. This is a puzzling effect, but you are setting up for a really surprising conclusion.

Take the pencil with your right hand and pretend to drop it down the jacket's left sleeve. Really you drop it into the inside jacket's left pocket.

Lower your left arm slowly. Shake it and allow the long pencil to slide down so that the eraser end hits your palm. Curl your left hand around the pencil. With your right hand *slowly* remove the pencil. Keep pulling it into view, Figure 185. The startling illusion is that the pencil has stretched to many times its original size! It is an astonishing trick.

Fig. 185.

A CATALOG OF SELECTED DOVER
BOOKS IN ALL FIELDS OF INTEREST

CONCERNING THE SPIRITUAL IN ART, Wassily Kandinsky. Pioneering work by father of abstract art. Thoughts on color theory, nature of art. Analysis of earlier masters. 12 illustrations. 80pp. of text. 5⅜ x 8½. 23411-8

ANIMALS: 1,419 Copyright-Free Illustrations of Mammals, Birds, Fish, Insects, etc., Jim Harter (ed.). Clear wood engravings present, in extremely lifelike poses, over 1,000 species of animals. One of the most extensive pictorial sourcebooks of its kind. Captions. Index. 284pp. 9 x 12. 23766-4

CELTIC ART: The Methods of Construction, George Bain. Simple geometric techniques for making Celtic interlacements, spirals, Kells-type initials, animals, humans, etc. Over 500 illustrations. 160pp. 9 x 12. (Available in U.S. only.) 22923-8

AN ATLAS OF ANATOMY FOR ARTISTS, Fritz Schider. Most thorough reference work on art anatomy in the world. Hundreds of illustrations, including selections from works by Vesalius, Leonardo, Goya, Ingres, Michelangelo, others. 593 illustrations. 192pp. 7⅛ x 10¼. 20241-0

CELTIC HAND STROKE-BY-STROKE (Irish Half-Uncial from "The Book of Kells"): An Arthur Baker Calligraphy Manual, Arthur Baker. Complete guide to creating each letter of the alphabet in distinctive Celtic manner. Covers hand position, strokes, pens, inks, paper, more. Illustrated. 48pp. 8¼ x 11. 24336-2

EASY ORIGAMI, John Montroll. Charming collection of 32 projects (hat, cup, pelican, piano, swan, many more) specially designed for the novice origami hobbyist. Clearly illustrated easy-to-follow instructions insure that even beginning papercrafters will achieve successful results. 48pp. 8¼ x 11. 27298-2

THE COMPLETE BOOK OF BIRDHOUSE CONSTRUCTION FOR WOODWORKERS, Scott D. Campbell. Detailed instructions, illustrations, tables. Also data on bird habitat and instinct patterns. Bibliography. 3 tables. 63 illustrations in 15 figures. 48pp. 5¼ x 8½. 24407-5

BLOOMINGDALE'S ILLUSTRATED 1886 CATALOG: Fashions, Dry Goods and Housewares, Bloomingdale Brothers. Famed merchants' extremely rare catalog depicting about 1,700 products: clothing, housewares, firearms, dry goods, jewelry, more. Invaluable for dating, identifying vintage items. Also, copyright-free graphics for artists, designers. Co-published with Henry Ford Museum & Greenfield Village. 160pp. 8¼ x 11. 25780-0

HISTORIC COSTUME IN PICTURES, Braun & Schneider. Over 1,450 costumed figures in clearly detailed engravings–from dawn of civilization to end of 19th century. Captions. Many folk costumes. 256pp. 8⅜ x 11¾. 23150-X

STICKLEY CRAFTSMAN FURNITURE CATALOGS, Gustav Stickley and L. & J. G. Stickley. Beautiful, functional furniture in two authentic catalogs from 1910. 594 illustrations, including 277 photos, show settles, rockers, armchairs, reclining chairs, bookcases, desks, tables. 183pp. 6½ x 9¼. 23838-5

AMERICAN LOCOMOTIVES IN HISTORIC PHOTOGRAPHS: 1858 to 1949, Ron Ziel (ed.). A rare collection of 126 meticulously detailed official photographs, called "builder portraits," of American locomotives that majestically chronicle the rise of steam locomotive power in America. Introduction. Detailed captions. xi+ 129pp. 9 x 12. 27393-8

AMERICA'S LIGHTHOUSES: An Illustrated History, Francis Ross Holland, Jr. Delightfully written, profusely illustrated fact-filled survey of over 200 American lighthouses since 1716. History, anecdotes, technological advances, more. 240pp. 8 x 10¾. 25576-X

TOWARDS A NEW ARCHITECTURE, Le Corbusier. Pioneering manifesto by founder of "International School." Technical and aesthetic theories, views of industry, economics, relation of form to function, "mass-production split" and much more. Profusely illustrated. 320pp. 6⅛ x 9¼. (Available in U.S. only.) 25023-7

HOW THE OTHER HALF LIVES, Jacob Riis. Famous journalistic record, exposing poverty and degradation of New York slums around 1900, by major social reformer. 100 striking and influential photographs. 233pp. 10 x 7⅞. 22012-5

FRUIT KEY AND TWIG KEY TO TREES AND SHRUBS, William M. Harlow. One of the handiest and most widely used identification aids. Fruit key covers 120 deciduous and evergreen species; twig key 160 deciduous species. Easily used. Over 300 photographs. 126pp. 5⅜ x 8½. 20511-8

COMMON BIRD SONGS, Dr. Donald J. Borror. Songs of 60 most common U.S. birds: robins, sparrows, cardinals, bluejays, finches, more–arranged in order of increasing complexity. Up to 9 variations of songs of each species.
Cassette and manual 99911-4

ORCHIDS AS HOUSE PLANTS, Rebecca Tyson Northen. Grow cattleyas and many other kinds of orchids–in a window, in a case, or under artificial light. 63 illustrations. 148pp. 5⅜ x 8½. 23261-1

MONSTER MAZES, Dave Phillips. Masterful mazes at four levels of difficulty. Avoid deadly perils and evil creatures to find magical treasures. Solutions for all 32 exciting illustrated puzzles. 48pp. 8¼ x 11. 26005-4

MOZART'S DON GIOVANNI (DOVER OPERA LIBRETTO SERIES), Wolfgang Amadeus Mozart. Introduced and translated by Ellen H. Bleiler. Standard Italian libretto, with complete English translation. Convenient and thoroughly portable–an ideal companion for reading along with a recording or the performance itself. Introduction. List of characters. Plot summary. 121pp. 5¼ x 8½. 24944-1

TECHNICAL MANUAL AND DICTIONARY OF CLASSICAL BALLET, Gail Grant. Defines, explains, comments on steps, movements, poses and concepts. 15-page pictorial section. Basic book for student, viewer. 127pp. 5⅜ x 8½. 21843-0

THE CLARINET AND CLARINET PLAYING, David Pino. Lively, comprehensive work features suggestions about technique, musicianship, and musical interpretation, as well as guidelines for teaching, making your own reeds, and preparing for public performance. Includes an intriguing look at clarinet history. "A godsend," *The Clarinet,* Journal of the International Clarinet Society. Appendixes. 7 illus. 320pp. 5⅜ x 8½. 40270-3

HOLLYWOOD GLAMOR PORTRAITS, John Kobal (ed.). 145 photos from 1926-49. Harlow, Gable, Bogart, Bacall; 94 stars in all. Full background on photographers, technical aspects. 160pp. 8⅜ x 11¼. 23352-9

THE ANNOTATED CASEY AT THE BAT: A Collection of Ballads about the Mighty Casey/Third, Revised Edition, Martin Gardner (ed.). Amusing sequels and parodies of one of America's best-loved poems: Casey's Revenge, Why Casey Whiffed, Casey's Sister at the Bat, others. 256pp. 5⅜ x 8½. 28598-7

THE RAVEN AND OTHER FAVORITE POEMS, Edgar Allan Poe. Over 40 of the author's most memorable poems: "The Bells," "Ulalume," "Israfel," "To Helen," "The Conqueror Worm," "Eldorado," "Annabel Lee," many more. Alphabetic lists of titles and first lines. 64pp. 5$\frac{3}{16}$ x 8¼. 26685-0

PERSONAL MEMOIRS OF U. S. GRANT, Ulysses Simpson Grant. Intelligent, deeply moving firsthand account of Civil War campaigns, considered by many the finest military memoirs ever written. Includes letters, historic photographs, maps and more. 528pp. 6⅛ x 9¼. 28587-1

ANCIENT EGYPTIAN MATERIALS AND INDUSTRIES, A. Lucas and J. Harris. Fascinating, comprehensive, thoroughly documented text describes this ancient civilization's vast resources and the processes that incorporated them in daily life, including the use of animal products, building materials, cosmetics, perfumes and incense, fibers, glazed ware, glass and its manufacture, materials used in the mummification process, and much more. 544pp. 6⅛ x 9¼. (Available in U.S. only.) 40446-3

RUSSIAN STORIES/RUSSKIE RASSKAZY: A Dual-Language Book, edited by Gleb Struve. Twelve tales by such masters as Chekhov, Tolstoy, Dostoevsky, Pushkin, others. Excellent word-for-word English translations on facing pages, plus teaching and study aids, Russian/English vocabulary, biographical/critical introductions, more. 416pp. 5⅜ x 8½. 26244-8

PHILADELPHIA THEN AND NOW: 60 Sites Photographed in the Past and Present, Kenneth Finkel and Susan Oyama. Rare photographs of City Hall, Logan Square, Independence Hall, Betsy Ross House, other landmarks juxtaposed with contemporary views. Captures changing face of historic city. Introduction. Captions. 128pp. 8¼ x 11. 25790-8

AIA ARCHITECTURAL GUIDE TO NASSAU AND SUFFOLK COUNTIES, LONG ISLAND, The American Institute of Architects, Long Island Chapter, and the Society for the Preservation of Long Island Antiquities. Comprehensive, well-researched and generously illustrated volume brings to life over three centuries of Long Island's great architectural heritage. More than 240 photographs with authoritative, extensively detailed captions. 176pp. 8¼ x 11. 26946-9

NORTH AMERICAN INDIAN LIFE: Customs and Traditions of 23 Tribes, Elsie Clews Parsons (ed.). 27 fictionalized essays by noted anthropologists examine religion, customs, government, additional facets of life among the Winnebago, Crow, Zuni, Eskimo, other tribes. 480pp. 6⅛ x 9¼. 27377-6

FRANK LLOYD WRIGHT'S DANA HOUSE, Donald Hoffmann. Pictorial essay of residential masterpiece with over 160 interior and exterior photos, plans, elevations, sketches and studies. 128pp. 9¼ x 10¾. 29120-0

THE MALE AND FEMALE FIGURE IN MOTION: 60 Classic Photographic Sequences, Eadweard Muybridge. 60 true-action photographs of men and women walking, running, climbing, bending, turning, etc., reproduced from rare 19th-century masterpiece. vi + 121pp. 9 x 12. 24745-7

1001 QUESTIONS ANSWERED ABOUT THE SEASHORE, N. J. Berrill and Jacquelyn Berrill. Queries answered about dolphins, sea snails, sponges, starfish, fishes, shore birds, many others. Covers appearance, breeding, growth, feeding, much more. 305pp. 5¼ x 8¼. 23366-9

ATTRACTING BIRDS TO YOUR YARD, William J. Weber. Easy-to-follow guide offers advice on how to attract the greatest diversity of birds: birdhouses, feeders, water and waterers, much more. 96pp. 5³⁄₁₆ x 8¼. 28927-3

MEDICINAL AND OTHER USES OF NORTH AMERICAN PLANTS: A Historical Survey with Special Reference to the Eastern Indian Tribes, Charlotte Erichsen-Brown. Chronological historical citations document 500 years of usage of plants, trees, shrubs native to eastern Canada, northeastern U.S. Also complete identifying information. 343 illustrations. 544pp. 6½ x 9¼. 25951-X

STORYBOOK MAZES, Dave Phillips. 23 stories and mazes on two-page spreads: Wizard of Oz, Treasure Island, Robin Hood, etc. Solutions. 64pp. 8¼ x 11. 23628-5

AMERICAN NEGRO SONGS: 230 Folk Songs and Spirituals, Religious and Secular, John W. Work. This authoritative study traces the African influences of songs sung and played by black Americans at work, in church, and as entertainment. The author discusses the lyric significance of such songs as "Swing Low, Sweet Chariot," "John Henry," and others and offers the words and music for 230 songs. Bibliography. Index of Song Titles. 272pp. 6½ x 9¼. 40271-1

MOVIE-STAR PORTRAITS OF THE FORTIES, John Kobal (ed.). 163 glamor, studio photos of 106 stars of the 1940s: Rita Hayworth, Ava Gardner, Marlon Brando, Clark Gable, many more. 176pp. 8⅜ x 11¼. 23546-7

BENCHLEY LOST AND FOUND, Robert Benchley. Finest humor from early 30s, about pet peeves, child psychologists, post office and others. Mostly unavailable elsewhere. 73 illustrations by Peter Arno and others. 183pp. 5⅜ x 8½. 22410-4

YEKL and THE IMPORTED BRIDEGROOM AND OTHER STORIES OF YIDDISH NEW YORK, Abraham Cahan. Film Hester Street based on Yekl (1896). Novel, other stories among first about Jewish immigrants on N.Y.'s East Side. 240pp. 5⅜ x 8½. 22427-9

SELECTED POEMS, Walt Whitman. Generous sampling from Leaves of Grass. Twenty-four poems include "I Hear America Singing," "Song of the Open Road," "I Sing the Body Electric," "When Lilacs Last in the Dooryard Bloom'd," "O Captain! My Captain!"–all reprinted from an authoritative edition. Lists of titles and first lines. 128pp. 5³⁄₁₆ x 8¼. 26878-0

THE BEST TALES OF HOFFMANN, E. T. A. Hoffmann. 10 of Hoffmann's most important stories: "Nutcracker and the King of Mice," "The Golden Flowerpot," etc. 458pp. 5⅜ x 8½.　　21793-0

FROM FETISH TO GOD IN ANCIENT EGYPT, E. A. Wallis Budge. Rich detailed survey of Egyptian conception of "God" and gods, magic, cult of animals, Osiris, more. Also, superb English translations of hymns and legends. 240 illustrations. 545pp. 5⅜ x 8½.　　25803-3

FRENCH STORIES/CONTES FRANÇAIS: A Dual-Language Book, Wallace Fowlie. Ten stories by French masters, Voltaire to Camus: "Micromegas" by Voltaire; "The Atheist's Mass" by Balzac; "Minuet" by de Maupassant; "The Guest" by Camus, six more. Excellent English translations on facing pages. Also French-English vocabulary list, exercises, more. 352pp. 5⅜ x 8½.　　26443-2

CHICAGO AT THE TURN OF THE CENTURY IN PHOTOGRAPHS: 122 Historic Views from the Collections of the Chicago Historical Society, Larry A. Viskochil. Rare large-format prints offer detailed views of City Hall, State Street, the Loop, Hull House, Union Station, many other landmarks, circa 1904-1913. Introduction. Captions. Maps. 144pp. 9⅜ x 12¼.　　24656-6

OLD BROOKLYN IN EARLY PHOTOGRAPHS, 1865-1929, William Lee Younger. Luna Park, Gravesend race track, construction of Grand Army Plaza, moving of Hotel Brighton, etc. 157 previously unpublished photographs. 165pp. 8⅞ x 11¾.　　23587-4

THE MYTHS OF THE NORTH AMERICAN INDIANS, Lewis Spence. Rich anthology of the myths and legends of the Algonquins, Iroquois, Pawnees and Sioux, prefaced by an extensive historical and ethnological commentary. 36 illustrations. 480pp. 5⅜ x 8½.　　25967-6

AN ENCYCLOPEDIA OF BATTLES: Accounts of Over 1,560 Battles from 1479 B.C. to the Present, David Eggenberger. Essential details of every major battle in recorded history from the first battle of Megiddo in 1479 B.C. to Grenada in 1984. List of Battle Maps. New Appendix covering the years 1967-1984. Index. 99 illustrations. 544pp. 6½ x 9¼.　　24913-1

SAILING ALONE AROUND THE WORLD, Captain Joshua Slocum. First man to sail around the world, alone, in small boat. One of great feats of seamanship told in delightful manner. 67 illustrations. 294pp. 5⅜ x 8½.　　20326-3

ANARCHISM AND OTHER ESSAYS, Emma Goldman. Powerful, penetrating, prophetic essays on direct action, role of minorities, prison reform, puritan hypocrisy, violence, etc. 271pp. 5⅜ x 8½.　　22484-8

MYTHS OF THE HINDUS AND BUDDHISTS, Ananda K. Coomaraswamy and Sister Nivedita. Great stories of the epics; deeds of Krishna, Shiva, taken from puranas, Vedas, folk tales; etc. 32 illustrations. 400pp. 5⅜ x 8½.　　21759-0

THE TRAUMA OF BIRTH, Otto Rank. Rank's controversial thesis that anxiety neurosis is caused by profound psychological trauma which occurs at birth. 256pp. 5⅜ x 8½.　　27974-X

A THEOLOGICO-POLITICAL TREATISE, Benedict Spinoza. Also contains unfinished Political Treatise. Great classic on religious liberty, theory of government on common consent. R. Elwes translation. Total of 421pp. 5⅜ x 8½.　　20249-6

MY BONDAGE AND MY FREEDOM, Frederick Douglass. Born a slave, Douglass became outspoken force in antislavery movement. The best of Douglass' autobiographies. Graphic description of slave life. 464pp. 5⅜ x 8½.   22457-0

FOLLOWING THE EQUATOR: A Journey Around the World, Mark Twain. Fascinating humorous account of 1897 voyage to Hawaii, Australia, India, New Zealand, etc. Ironic, bemused reports on peoples, customs, climate, flora and fauna, politics, much more. 197 illustrations. 720pp. 5⅜ x 8½.   26113-1

THE PEOPLE CALLED SHAKERS, Edward D. Andrews. Definitive study of Shakers: origins, beliefs, practices, dances, social organization, furniture and crafts, etc. 33 illustrations. 351pp. 5⅜ x 8½.   21081-2

THE MYTHS OF GREECE AND ROME, H. A. Guerber. A classic of mythology, generously illustrated, long prized for its simple, graphic, accurate retelling of the principal myths of Greece and Rome, and for its commentary on their origins and significance. With 64 illustrations by Michelangelo, Raphael, Titian, Rubens, Canova, Bernini and others. 480pp. 5⅜ x 8½.   27584-1

PSYCHOLOGY OF MUSIC, Carl E. Seashore. Classic work discusses music as a medium from psychological viewpoint. Clear treatment of physical acoustics, auditory apparatus, sound perception, development of musical skills, nature of musical feeling, host of other topics. 88 figures. 408pp. 5⅜ x 8½.   21851-1

THE PHILOSOPHY OF HISTORY, Georg W. Hegel. Great classic of Western thought develops concept that history is not chance but rational process, the evolution of freedom. 457pp. 5⅜ x 8½.   20112-0

THE BOOK OF TEA, Kakuzo Okakura. Minor classic of the Orient: entertaining, charming explanation, interpretation of traditional Japanese culture in terms of tea ceremony. 94pp. 5⅜ x 8½.   20070-1

LIFE IN ANCIENT EGYPT, Adolf Erman. Fullest, most thorough, detailed older account with much not in more recent books, domestic life, religion, magic, medicine, commerce, much more. Many illustrations reproduce tomb paintings, carvings, hieroglyphs, etc. 597pp. 5⅜ x 8½.   22632-8

SUNDIALS, Their Theory and Construction, Albert Waugh. Far and away the best, most thorough coverage of ideas, mathematics concerned, types, construction, adjusting anywhere. Simple, nontechnical treatment allows even children to build several of these dials. Over 100 illustrations. 230pp. 5⅜ x 8½.   22947-5

THEORETICAL HYDRODYNAMICS, L. M. Milne-Thomson. Classic exposition of the mathematical theory of fluid motion, applicable to both hydrodynamics and aerodynamics. Over 600 exercises. 768pp. 6⅛ x 9¼.   68970-0

SONGS OF EXPERIENCE: Facsimile Reproduction with 26 Plates in Full Color, William Blake. 26 full-color plates from a rare 1826 edition. Includes "The Tyger," "London," "Holy Thursday," and other poems. Printed text of poems. 48pp. 5¼ x 7.   24636-1

OLD-TIME VIGNETTES IN FULL COLOR, Carol Belanger Grafton (ed.). Over 390 charming, often sentimental illustrations, selected from archives of Victorian graphics—pretty women posing, children playing, food, flowers, kittens and puppies, smiling cherubs, birds and butterflies, much more. All copyright-free. 48pp. 9¼ x 12¼.   27269-9

PERSPECTIVE FOR ARTISTS, Rex Vicat Cole. Depth, perspective of sky and sea, shadows, much more, not usually covered. 391 diagrams, 81 reproductions of drawings and paintings. 279pp. 5⅜ x 8½. 22487-2

DRAWING THE LIVING FIGURE, Joseph Sheppard. Innovative approach to artistic anatomy focuses on specifics of surface anatomy, rather than muscles and bones. Over 170 drawings of live models in front, back and side views, and in widely varying poses. Accompanying diagrams. 177 illustrations. Introduction. Index. 144pp. 8⅜ x11¼. 26723-7

GOTHIC AND OLD ENGLISH ALPHABETS: 100 Complete Fonts, Dan X. Solo. Add power, elegance to posters, signs, other graphics with 100 stunning copyright-free alphabets: Blackstone, Dolbey, Germania, 97 more–including many lower-case, numerals, punctuation marks. 104pp. 8⅛ x 11. 24695-7

HOW TO DO BEADWORK, Mary White. Fundamental book on craft from simple projects to five-bead chains and woven works. 106 illustrations. 142pp. 5⅜ x 8. 20697-1

THE BOOK OF WOOD CARVING, Charles Marshall Sayers. Finest book for beginners discusses fundamentals and offers 34 designs. "Absolutely first rate . . . well thought out and well executed."–E. J. Tangerman. 118pp. 7¾ x 10⅝. 23654-4

ILLUSTRATED CATALOG OF CIVIL WAR MILITARY GOODS: Union Army Weapons, Insignia, Uniform Accessories, and Other Equipment, Schuyler, Hartley, and Graham. Rare, profusely illustrated 1846 catalog includes Union Army uniform and dress regulations, arms and ammunition, coats, insignia, flags, swords, rifles, etc. 226 illustrations. 160pp. 9 x 12. 24939-5

WOMEN'S FASHIONS OF THE EARLY 1900s: An Unabridged Republication of "New York Fashions, 1909," National Cloak & Suit Co. Rare catalog of mail-order fashions documents women's and children's clothing styles shortly after the turn of the century. Captions offer full descriptions, prices. Invaluable resource for fashion, costume historians. Approximately 725 illustrations. 128pp. 8⅜ x 11¼. 27276-1

THE 1912 AND 1915 GUSTAV STICKLEY FURNITURE CATALOGS, Gustav Stickley. With over 200 detailed illustrations and descriptions, these two catalogs are essential reading and reference materials and identification guides for Stickley furniture. Captions cite materials, dimensions and prices. 112pp. 6½ x 9¼. 26676-1

EARLY AMERICAN LOCOMOTIVES, John H. White, Jr. Finest locomotive engravings from early 19th century: historical (1804–74), main-line (after 1870), special, foreign, etc. 147 plates. 142pp. 11⅜ x 8¼. 22772-3

THE TALL SHIPS OF TODAY IN PHOTOGRAPHS, Frank O. Braynard. Lavishly illustrated tribute to nearly 100 majestic contemporary sailing vessels: Amerigo Vespucci, Clearwater, Constitution, Eagle, Mayflower, Sea Cloud, Victory, many more. Authoritative captions provide statistics, background on each ship. 190 black-and-white photographs and illustrations. Introduction. 128pp. 8⅞ x 11¾. 27163-3

LITTLE BOOK OF EARLY AMERICAN CRAFTS AND TRADES, Peter Stockham (ed.). 1807 children's book explains crafts and trades: baker, hatter, cooper, potter, and many others. 23 copperplate illustrations. 140pp. 4⅝ x 6. 23336-7

VICTORIAN FASHIONS AND COSTUMES FROM HARPER'S BAZAR, 1867–1898, Stella Blum (ed.). Day costumes, evening wear, sports clothes, shoes, hats, other accessories in over 1,000 detailed engravings. 320pp. 9⅜ x 12¼. 22990-4

GUSTAV STICKLEY, THE CRAFTSMAN, Mary Ann Smith. Superb study surveys broad scope of Stickley's achievement, especially in architecture. Design philosophy, rise and fall of the Craftsman empire, descriptions and floor plans for many Craftsman houses, more. 86 black-and-white halftones. 31 line illustrations. Introduction 208pp. 6½ x 9¼. 27210-9

THE LONG ISLAND RAIL ROAD IN EARLY PHOTOGRAPHS, Ron Ziel. Over 220 rare photos, informative text document origin (1844) and development of rail service on Long Island. Vintage views of early trains, locomotives, stations, passengers, crews, much more. Captions. 8⅞ x 11¾. 26301-0

VOYAGE OF THE LIBERDADE, Joshua Slocum. Great 19th-century mariner's thrilling, first-hand account of the wreck of his ship off South America, the 35-foot boat he built from the wreckage, and its remarkable voyage home. 128pp. 5⅜ x 8½. 40022-0

TEN BOOKS ON ARCHITECTURE, Vitruvius. The most important book ever written on architecture. Early Roman aesthetics, technology, classical orders, site selection, all other aspects. Morgan translation. 331pp. 5⅜ x 8½. 20645-9

THE HUMAN FIGURE IN MOTION, Eadweard Muybridge. More than 4,500 stopped-action photos, in action series, showing undraped men, women, children jumping, lying down, throwing, sitting, wrestling, carrying, etc. 390pp. 7⅞ x 10⅝. 20204-6 Clothbd.

TREES OF THE EASTERN AND CENTRAL UNITED STATES AND CANADA, William M. Harlow. Best one-volume guide to 140 trees. Full descriptions, woodlore, range, etc. Over 600 illustrations. Handy size. 288pp. 4½ x 6⅜. 20395-6

SONGS OF WESTERN BIRDS, Dr. Donald J. Borror. Complete song and call repertoire of 60 western species, including flycatchers, juncoes, cactus wrens, many more–includes fully illustrated booklet. Cassette and manual 99913-0

GROWING AND USING HERBS AND SPICES, Milo Miloradovich. Versatile handbook provides all the information needed for cultivation and use of all the herbs and spices available in North America. 4 illustrations. Index. Glossary. 236pp. 5⅜ x 8½. 25058-X

BIG BOOK OF MAZES AND LABYRINTHS, Walter Shepherd. 50 mazes and labyrinths in all–classical, solid, ripple, and more–in one great volume. Perfect inexpensive puzzler for clever youngsters. Full solutions. 112pp. 8⅛ x 11. 22951-3

PIANO TUNING, J. Cree Fischer. Clearest, best book for beginner, amateur. Simple repairs, raising dropped notes, tuning by easy method of flattened fifths. No previous skills needed. 4 illustrations. 201pp. 5⅜ x 8½. 23267-0

HINTS TO SINGERS, Lillian Nordica. Selecting the right teacher, developing confidence, overcoming stage fright, and many other important skills receive thoughtful discussion in this indispensible guide, written by a world-famous diva of four decades' experience. 96pp. 5⅜ x 8½. 40094-8

THE COMPLETE NONSENSE OF EDWARD LEAR, Edward Lear. All nonsense limericks, zany alphabets, Owl and Pussycat, songs, nonsense botany, etc., illustrated by Lear. Total of 320pp. 5⅜ x 8½. (Available in U.S. only.) 20167-8

VICTORIAN PARLOUR POETRY: An Annotated Anthology, Michael R. Turner. 117 gems by Longfellow, Tennyson, Browning, many lesser-known poets. "The Village Blacksmith," "Curfew Must Not Ring Tonight," "Only a Baby Small," dozens more, often difficult to find elsewhere. Index of poets, titles, first lines. xxiii + 325pp. 5⅝ x 8¼. 27044-0

DUBLINERS, James Joyce. Fifteen stories offer vivid, tightly focused observations of the lives of Dublin's poorer classes. At least one, "The Dead," is considered a masterpiece. Reprinted complete and unabridged from standard edition. 160pp. 5$\frac{3}{16}$ x 8¼. 26870-5

GREAT WEIRD TALES: 14 Stories by Lovecraft, Blackwood, Machen and Others, S. T. Joshi (ed.). 14 spellbinding tales, including "The Sin Eater," by Fiona McLeod, "The Eye Above the Mantel," by Frank Belknap Long, as well as renowned works by R. H. Barlow, Lord Dunsany, Arthur Machen, W. C. Morrow and eight other masters of the genre. 256pp. 5⅜ x 8½. (Available in U.S. only.) 40436-6

THE BOOK OF THE SACRED MAGIC OF ABRAMELIN THE MAGE, translated by S. MacGregor Mathers. Medieval manuscript of ceremonial magic. Basic document in Aleister Crowley, Golden Dawn groups. 268pp. 5⅜ x 8½. 23211-5

NEW RUSSIAN-ENGLISH AND ENGLISH-RUSSIAN DICTIONARY, M. A. O'Brien. This is a remarkably handy Russian dictionary, containing a surprising amount of information, including over 70,000 entries. 366pp. 4½ x 6⅛. 20208-9

HISTORIC HOMES OF THE AMERICAN PRESIDENTS, Second, Revised Edition, Irvin Haas. A traveler's guide to American Presidential homes, most open to the public, depicting and describing homes occupied by every American President from George Washington to George Bush. With visiting hours, admission charges, travel routes. 175 photographs. Index. 160pp. 8¼ x 11. 26751-2

NEW YORK IN THE FORTIES, Andreas Feininger. 162 brilliant photographs by the well-known photographer, formerly with *Life* magazine. Commuters, shoppers, Times Square at night, much else from city at its peak. Captions by John von Hartz. 181pp. 9¼ x 10¾. 23585-8

INDIAN SIGN LANGUAGE, William Tomkins. Over 525 signs developed by Sioux and other tribes. Written instructions and diagrams. Also 290 pictographs. 111pp. 6⅛ x 9¼. 22029-X

ANATOMY: A Complete Guide for Artists, Joseph Sheppard. A master of figure drawing shows artists how to render human anatomy convincingly. Over 460 illustrations. 224pp. 8⅜ x 11¼. 27279-6

MEDIEVAL CALLIGRAPHY: Its History and Technique, Marc Drogin. Spirited history, comprehensive instruction manual covers 13 styles (ca. 4th century through 15th). Excellent photographs; directions for duplicating medieval techniques with modern tools. 224pp. 8⅜ x 11¼. 26142-5

DRIED FLOWERS: How to Prepare Them, Sarah Whitlock and Martha Rankin. Complete instructions on how to use silica gel, meal and borax, perlite aggregate, sand and borax, glycerine and water to create attractive permanent flower arrangements. 12 illustrations. 32pp. 5⅜ x 8½. 21802-3

EASY-TO-MAKE BIRD FEEDERS FOR WOODWORKERS, Scott D. Campbell. Detailed, simple-to-use guide for designing, constructing, caring for and using feeders. Text, illustrations for 12 classic and contemporary designs. 96pp. 5⅜ x 8½. 25847-5

SCOTTISH WONDER TALES FROM MYTH AND LEGEND, Donald A. Mackenzie. 16 lively tales tell of giants rumbling down mountainsides, of a magic wand that turns stone pillars into warriors, of gods and goddesses, evil hags, powerful forces and more. 240pp. 5⅜ x 8½. 29677-6

THE HISTORY OF UNDERCLOTHES, C. Willett Cunnington and Phyllis Cunnington. Fascinating, well-documented survey covering six centuries of English undergarments, enhanced with over 100 illustrations: 12th-century laced-up bodice, footed long drawers (1795), 19th-century bustles, 19th-century corsets for men, Victorian "bust improvers," much more. 272pp. 5⅜ x 8¼. 27124-2

ARTS AND CRAFTS FURNITURE: The Complete Brooks Catalog of 1912, Brooks Manufacturing Co. Photos and detailed descriptions of more than 150 now very collectible furniture designs from the Arts and Crafts movement depict davenports, settees, buffets, desks, tables, chairs, bedsteads, dressers and more, all built of solid, quarter-sawed oak. Invaluable for students and enthusiasts of antiques, Americana and the decorative arts. 80pp. 6½ x 9¼. 27471-3

WILBUR AND ORVILLE: A Biography of the Wright Brothers, Fred Howard. Definitive, crisply written study tells the full story of the brothers' lives and work. A vividly written biography, unparalleled in scope and color, that also captures the spirit of an extraordinary era. 560pp. 6⅛ x 9¼. 40297-5

THE ARTS OF THE SAILOR: Knotting, Splicing and Ropework, Hervey Garrett Smith. Indispensable shipboard reference covers tools, basic knots and useful hitches; handsewing and canvas work, more. Over 100 illustrations. Delightful reading for sea lovers. 256pp. 5⅜ x 8½. 26440-8

FRANK LLOYD WRIGHT'S FALLINGWATER: The House and Its History, Second, Revised Edition, Donald Hoffmann. A total revision–both in text and illustrations–of the standard document on Fallingwater, the boldest, most personal architectural statement of Wright's mature years, updated with valuable new material from the recently opened Frank Lloyd Wright Archives. "Fascinating"–*The New York Times*. 116 illustrations. 128pp. 9¼ x 10¾. 27430-6

PHOTOGRAPHIC SKETCHBOOK OF THE CIVIL WAR, Alexander Gardner. 100 photos taken on field during the Civil War. Famous shots of Manassas Harper's Ferry, Lincoln, Richmond, slave pens, etc. 244pp. 10⅝ x 8¼. 22731-6

FIVE ACRES AND INDEPENDENCE, Maurice G. Kains. Great back-to-the-land classic explains basics of self-sufficient farming. The one book to get. 95 illustrations. 397pp. 5⅜ x 8½. 20974-1

SONGS OF EASTERN BIRDS, Dr. Donald J. Borror. Songs and calls of 60 species most common to eastern U.S.: warblers, woodpeckers, flycatchers, thrushes, larks, many more in high-quality recording. Cassette and manual 99912-2

A MODERN HERBAL, Margaret Grieve. Much the fullest, most exact, most useful compilation of herbal material. Gigantic alphabetical encyclopedia, from aconite to zedoary, gives botanical information, medical properties, folklore, economic uses, much else. Indispensable to serious reader. 161 illustrations. 888pp. 6½ x 9¼. 2-vol. set. (Available in U.S. only.) Vol. I: 22798-7
Vol. II: 22799-5

HIDDEN TREASURE MAZE BOOK, Dave Phillips. Solve 34 challenging mazes accompanied by heroic tales of adventure. Evil dragons, people-eating plants, blood-thirsty giants, many more dangerous adversaries lurk at every twist and turn. 34 mazes, stories, solutions. 48pp. 8¼ x 11. 24566-7

LETTERS OF W. A. MOZART, Wolfgang A. Mozart. Remarkable letters show bawdy wit, humor, imagination, musical insights, contemporary musical world; includes some letters from Leopold Mozart. 276pp. 5⅜ x 8½. 22859-2

BASIC PRINCIPLES OF CLASSICAL BALLET, Agrippina Vaganova. Great Russian theoretician, teacher explains methods for teaching classical ballet. 118 illustrations. 175pp. 5⅜ x 8½. 22036-2

THE JUMPING FROG, Mark Twain. Revenge edition. The original story of The Celebrated Jumping Frog of Calaveras County, a hapless French translation, and Twain's hilarious "retranslation" from the French. 12 illustrations. 66pp. 5⅜ x 8½. 22686-7

BEST REMEMBERED POEMS, Martin Gardner (ed.). The 126 poems in this superb collection of 19th- and 20th-century British and American verse range from Shelley's "To a Skylark" to the impassioned "Renascence" of Edna St. Vincent Millay and to Edward Lear's whimsical "The Owl and the Pussycat." 224pp. 5⅜ x 8½. 27165-X

COMPLETE SONNETS, William Shakespeare. Over 150 exquisite poems deal with love, friendship, the tyranny of time, beauty's evanescence, death and other themes in language of remarkable power, precision and beauty. Glossary of archaic terms. 80pp. 5³⁄₁₆ x 8¼. 26686-9

THE BATTLES THAT CHANGED HISTORY, Fletcher Pratt. Eminent historian profiles 16 crucial conflicts, ancient to modern, that changed the course of civilization. 352pp. 5⅜ x 8½. 41129-X

THE WIT AND HUMOR OF OSCAR WILDE, Alvin Redman (ed.). More than 1,000 ripostes, paradoxes, wisecracks: Work is the curse of the drinking classes; I can resist everything except temptation; etc. 258pp. 5⅜ x 8½. 20602-5

SHAKESPEARE LEXICON AND QUOTATION DICTIONARY, Alexander Schmidt. Full definitions, locations, shades of meaning in every word in plays and poems. More than 50,000 exact quotations. 1,485pp. 6½ x 9¼. 2-vol. set.
Vol. 1: 22726-X
Vol. 2: 22727-8

SELECTED POEMS, Emily Dickinson. Over 100 best-known, best-loved poems by one of America's foremost poets, reprinted from authoritative early editions. No comparable edition at this price. Index of first lines. 64pp. 5³⁄₁₆ x 8¼. 26466-1

THE INSIDIOUS DR. FU-MANCHU, Sax Rohmer. The first of the popular mystery series introduces a pair of English detectives to their archnemesis, the diabolical Dr. Fu-Manchu. Flavorful atmosphere, fast-paced action, and colorful characters enliven this classic of the genre. 208pp. 5³⁄₁₆ x 8¼. 29898-1

THE MALLEUS MALEFICARUM OF KRAMER AND SPRENGER, translated by Montague Summers. Full text of most important witchhunter's "bible," used by both Catholics and Protestants. 278pp. 6⅝ x 10. 22802-9

SPANISH STORIES/CUENTOS ESPAÑOLES: A Dual-Language Book, Angel Flores (ed.). Unique format offers 13 great stories in Spanish by Cervantes, Borges, others. Faithful English translations on facing pages. 352pp. 5⅜ x 8½. 25399-6

GARDEN CITY, LONG ISLAND, IN EARLY PHOTOGRAPHS, 1869–1919, Mildred H. Smith. Handsome treasury of 118 vintage pictures, accompanied by carefully researched captions, document the Garden City Hotel fire (1899), the Vanderbilt Cup Race (1908), the first airmail flight departing from the Nassau Boulevard Aerodrome (1911), and much more. 96pp. 8⅞ x 11¾. 40669-5

OLD QUEENS, N.Y., IN EARLY PHOTOGRAPHS, Vincent F. Seyfried and William Asadorian. Over 160 rare photographs of Maspeth, Jamaica, Jackson Heights, and other areas. Vintage views of DeWitt Clinton mansion, 1939 World's Fair and more. Captions. 192pp. 8⅞ x 11. 26358-4

CAPTURED BY THE INDIANS: 15 Firsthand Accounts, 1750-1870, Frederick Drimmer. Astounding true historical accounts of grisly torture, bloody conflicts, relentless pursuits, miraculous escapes and more, by people who lived to tell the tale. 384pp. 5⅜ x 8½. 24901-8

THE WORLD'S GREAT SPEECHES (Fourth Enlarged Edition), Lewis Copeland, Lawrence W. Lamm, and Stephen J. McKenna. Nearly 300 speeches provide public speakers with a wealth of updated quotes and inspiration–from Pericles' funeral oration and William Jennings Bryan's "Cross of Gold Speech" to Malcolm X's powerful words on the Black Revolution and Earl of Spenser's tribute to his sister, Diana, Princess of Wales. 944pp. 5⅜ x 8⅜. 40903-1

THE BOOK OF THE SWORD, Sir Richard F. Burton. Great Victorian scholar/adventurer's eloquent, erudite history of the "queen of weapons"–from prehistory to early Roman Empire. Evolution and development of early swords, variations (sabre, broadsword, cutlass, scimitar, etc.), much more. 336pp. 6⅛ x 9¼.
25434-8

AUTOBIOGRAPHY: The Story of My Experiments with Truth, Mohandas K. Gandhi. Boyhood, legal studies, purification, the growth of the Satyagraha (nonviolent protest) movement. Critical, inspiring work of the man responsible for the freedom of India. 480pp. 5⅜ x 8½. (Available in U.S. only.) 24593-4

CELTIC MYTHS AND LEGENDS, T. W. Rolleston. Masterful retelling of Irish and Welsh stories and tales. Cuchulain, King Arthur, Deirdre, the Grail, many more. First paperback edition. 58 full-page illustrations. 512pp. 5⅜ x 8½. 26507-2

THE PRINCIPLES OF PSYCHOLOGY, William James. Famous long course complete, unabridged. Stream of thought, time perception, memory, experimental methods; great work decades ahead of its time. 94 figures. 1,391pp. 5⅜ x 8½. 2-vol. set. Vol. I: 20381-6 Vol. II: 20382-4

THE WORLD AS WILL AND REPRESENTATION, Arthur Schopenhauer. Definitive English translation of Schopenhauer's life work, correcting more than 1,000 errors, omissions in earlier translations. Translated by E. F. J. Payne. Total of 1,269pp. 5⅜ x 8½. 2-vol. set. Vol. 1: 21761-2 Vol. 2: 21762-0

MAGIC AND MYSTERY IN TIBET, Madame Alexandra David-Neel. Experiences among lamas, magicians, sages, sorcerers, Bonpa wizards. A true psychic discovery. 32 illustrations. 321pp. 5⅜ x 8½. (Available in U.S. only.) 22682-4

THE EGYPTIAN BOOK OF THE DEAD, E. A. Wallis Budge. Complete reproduction of Ani's papyrus, finest ever found. Full hieroglyphic text, interlinear transliteration, word-for-word translation, smooth translation. 533pp. 6½ x 9¼. 21866-X

MATHEMATICS FOR THE NONMATHEMATICIAN, Morris Kline. Detailed, college-level treatment of mathematics in cultural and historical context, with numerous exercises. Recommended Reading Lists. Tables. Numerous figures. 641pp. 5⅜ x 8½. 24823-2

PROBABILISTIC METHODS IN THE THEORY OF STRUCTURES, Isaac Elishakoff. Well-written introduction covers the elements of the theory of probability from two or more random variables, the reliability of such multivariable structures, the theory of random function, Monte Carlo methods of treating problems incapable of exact solution, and more. Examples. 502pp. 5⅜ x 8½. 40691-1

THE RIME OF THE ANCIENT MARINER, Gustave Doré, S. T. Coleridge. Doré's finest work; 34 plates capture moods, subtleties of poem. Flawless full-size reproductions printed on facing pages with authoritative text of poem. "Beautiful. Simply beautiful."–*Publisher's Weekly.* 77pp. 9¼ x 12. 22305-1

NORTH AMERICAN INDIAN DESIGNS FOR ARTISTS AND CRAFTSPEOPLE, Eva Wilson. Over 360 authentic copyright-free designs adapted from Navajo blankets, Hopi pottery, Sioux buffalo hides, more. Geometrics, symbolic figures, plant and animal motifs, etc. 128pp. 8⅜ x 11. (Not for sale in the United Kingdom.) 25341-4

SCULPTURE: Principles and Practice, Louis Slobodkin. Step-by-step approach to clay, plaster, metals, stone; classical and modern. 253 drawings, photos. 255pp. 8⅛ x 11. 22960-2

THE INFLUENCE OF SEA POWER UPON HISTORY, 1660–1783, A. T. Mahan. Influential classic of naval history and tactics still used as text in war colleges. First paperback edition. 4 maps. 24 battle plans. 640pp. 5⅜ x 8½. 25509-3

THE STORY OF THE TITANIC AS TOLD BY ITS SURVIVORS, Jack Winocour (ed.). What it was really like. Panic, despair, shocking inefficiency, and a little heroism. More thrilling than any fictional account. 26 illustrations. 320pp. 5⅜ x 8½. 20610-6

FAIRY AND FOLK TALES OF THE IRISH PEASANTRY, William Butler Yeats (ed.). Treasury of 64 tales from the twilight world of Celtic myth and legend: "The Soul Cages," "The Kildare Pooka," "King O'Toole and his Goose," many more. Introduction and Notes by W. B. Yeats. 352pp. 5⅜ x 8½. 26941-8

BUDDHIST MAHAYANA TEXTS, E. B. Cowell and others (eds.). Superb, accurate translations of basic documents in Mahayana Buddhism, highly important in history of religions. The Buddha-karita of Asvaghosha, Larger Sukhavativyuha, more. 448pp. 5⅜ x 8½. 25552-2

ONE TWO THREE . . . INFINITY: Facts and Speculations of Science, George Gamow. Great physicist's fascinating, readable overview of contemporary science: number theory, relativity, fourth dimension, entropy, genes, atomic structure, much more. 128 illustrations. Index. 352pp. 5⅜ x 8½. 25664-2

EXPERIMENTATION AND MEASUREMENT, W. J. Youden. Introductory manual explains laws of measurement in simple terms and offers tips for achieving accuracy and minimizing errors. Mathematics of measurement, use of instruments, experimenting with machines. 1994 edition. Foreword. Preface. Introduction. Epilogue. Selected Readings. Glossary. Index. Tables and figures. 128pp. 5⅜ x 8½. 40451-X

DALÍ ON MODERN ART: The Cuckolds of Antiquated Modern Art, Salvador Dalí. Influential painter skewers modern art and its practitioners. Outrageous evaluations of Picasso, Cézanne, Turner, more. 15 renderings of paintings discussed. 44 calligraphic decorations by Dalí. 96pp. 5⅜ x 8½. (Available in U.S. only.) 29220-7

ANTIQUE PLAYING CARDS: A Pictorial History, Henry René D'Allemagne. Over 900 elaborate, decorative images from rare playing cards (14th–20th centuries): Bacchus, death, dancing dogs, hunting scenes, royal coats of arms, players cheating, much more. 96pp. 9¼ x 12¼. 29265-7

MAKING FURNITURE MASTERPIECES: 30 Projects with Measured Drawings, Franklin H. Gottshall. Step-by-step instructions, illustrations for constructing handsome, useful pieces, among them a Sheraton desk, Chippendale chair, Spanish desk, Queen Anne table and a William and Mary dressing mirror. 224pp. 8⅛ x 11¼. 29338-6

THE FOSSIL BOOK: A Record of Prehistoric Life, Patricia V. Rich et al. Profusely illustrated definitive guide covers everything from single-celled organisms and dinosaurs to birds and mammals and the interplay between climate and man. Over 1,500 illustrations. 760pp. 7½ x 10⅛. 29371-8

Paperbound unless otherwise indicated. Available at your book dealer, online at **www.doverpublications.com**, or by writing to Dept. GI, Dover Publications, Inc., 31 East 2nd Street, Mineola, NY 11501. For current price information or for free catalogues (please indicate field of interest), write to Dover Publications or log on to **www.doverpublications.com** and see every Dover book in print. Dover publishes more than 500 books each year on science, elementary and advanced mathematics, biology, music, art, literary history, social sciences, and other areas.